How to Build A Winning Team

And Have Fun Doing It!

To George.

Best o'

Pete

Client Responses to the Process Described in This Book

Thanks very much for an exceptionally interesting and productive "Team Building" session with the Division of Forestry's senior staff!... My staff was unanimous in their assessment of the value of the time we spent with you: outstanding experience!... You have definitely earned a high degree of respect from me and my staff. This translated into a high comfort level, which in turn made for a very productive session.

Pete, on behalf of the Division's senior staff, we are all looking forward to a follow-up session with you to renew and expand our progress toward forging a strong management team.

Director of Forestry from a southern state

...Taking 20 key employees from the bank at one time was a major effort but one certainly worthwhile. Your focus on team building was good. Several of our folks have already commented on what they learned from this train-

ing. The time spent will surely help build a better team and a better bank.

From a bank president & CEO

You have demonstrated the ability to present timely management development training at every level of our organization – from our first goal setting/performance training to executive management to the recent team building training. You have gained the confidence and respect of our organization from top to bottom.

I look forward to a continuing partnership in our development program.

**From a major Japanese corporation
with world-wide operations**

...The simultaneously simple and extremely complex nature of human communication, especially in our international environment, becomes a more comfortable process to us daily as we practice improving methods.

Our follow-up training in teamwork has created a more cohesive organization quite capable of facing the gremlins of organizational destruction...

From a Fortune 500 manufacturing company

...Looking back at the progress our group has made, I don't like to think where we might have been today if we had not put into effect your team building program. All of us want to say a big "thank you." It was the best investment we ever made. The program is working...

**From a senior manager in a major
oil and gas company**

How to Build A Winning Team

And Have Fun Doing It!

by

Peter A. Land

SKYWARD PUBLISHING, INC.

Dallas, Texas

www.skywardpublishing.com

skyward@sheltonbbs.com

Copyright 2002, Skyward Publishing, Inc.

Publisher: Skyward Publishing, Inc.
               Dallas, Texas
               Marketing:
               813 Michael
               Kennett, MO 63857
               Phone/Fax (573) 717-1040
                E-Mail: skyward@sheltonbbs.com
               Web Site: www.skywardpublishing.com

Library of Congress Cataloging-in-Publication Data

Land, Peter, A.
    How to build a winning team (and have fun doing it!) by Peter A. Land.
        p. cm.
    Includes bibliographical references.
    ISBN 1-881554-14-7
    1.Teams in the workplace. I. Title.
HD66 .L36 2001
658.4'02–dc 21

                                                    2001020587

On September 26, 1998, my sister, Martha Land Lane, was killed in an automobile accident in North Carolina. Marty did everything with dignity and class — a loving wife and mother, a wonderful grandmother, a devoted church leader, an effective civic leader, and a great friend. She was admired and respected at every level in the community. Waitresses, shopkeepers, bank presidents, and the Governor of North Carolina attended her funeral.

I dedicate this book to her loving memory.

Table of Contents

Acknowledgments

Writing a book is such a personally engrossing experience that it is easy to lose sight of one major premise—this book is written for you, not me. I have asked several talented colleagues to proofread and critique this book on your behalf. They did an honest and devoted job of representing you—the reader and ultimate beneficiary of this book.

Once again I turned to a few friends whose suggestions helped my first book, *Managing to Get the Job Done*, to be selected by the Newbridge Executive Book Club as an alternate selection in 1994: Gail Kelley-Webb, Bill Land, Beth Land Cookston, and Jay McAuley. Francis Micale, a major trainer, consultant, author and colleague in Atlanta shared her insightful ideas, which strengthened the manuscript. My dear friend and master of the English language, Chapman Greer, worked her magic on this book, too.

The Gold Medal for Insight and Advice goes to Dr. Dick Leatherman, Chairman of International Training Consultants, Inc., in Richmond, VA. He has forgotten more about training than I will ever know.

Dick has been a mentor, colleague, and friend for over 15 years. I have used his excellent training materials with great success because they are grounded in solid theory and, more importantly, they teach the critical skill sets needed to be successful in management.

Finally, a special thank you to our administrative assistant, Barbara Hailes, who stayed committed and enthusiastic after the many rewrites and revisions; thank you for your wonderful support.

Introduction

Over the past forty years, I have seen hundreds of teams form, function, and fade. There is a unique chemistry which welds diverse personalities, skills, and needs into the strong, cohesive human phenomenon we call "teams." One of the distinguishing characteristics of teams is that they all *DO* something; they tend to be known by their accomplishments. From my personal experience as an active team member and leader, plus many years of study and consulting, I believe I understand the true elements, characteristics, and skills which allow some teams to achieve excellence by every measure of merit, while similar groups never quite earn that badge of honor — A Winning Team.

The purpose of this book is to share with you not only the insights I have gained but also the specific skills and techniques you can use as a formal or informal team leader to accomplish far greater goals than you ever dreamed possible.

In my first book, *Managing to Get the Job Done*, John Wiley & Sons, 1994, I discussed the relationship between the performance variables of Readiness (Resources), Willingness (Motivation), Ability (Skills), and Performance (Profits/Productivity). The formula, $RxWxA = P$ explains that those variables interact in a multiplicative fashion. Therefore, if any one of the elements of Readiness, Willingness, or Ability is suppressed, then the final output is affected in the same manner. This formula works particularly well with teams — whether in sports, business, the military, government, or non-profit organizations.

Teamwork: A Newcomer to the Scene

Books about team building and coaching abound in the management literature today; however, teamwork is a relative newcomer to the management scene. While athletic teams have been studied and admired for generations, I have come to believe strongly that the same characteristics, elements, and skills which contribute to winning Super Bowls, World Series, and Gold Medals can, when applied properly, help businesses gain market share, discover new products, and enhance stockholder equity.

You will notice that the first portion of this book makes several references to athletic teams and their coaches. The purpose is to familiarize all readers, even those who have had limited personal experience with team sports, to the subtle but important values and "team mentality" inherent in athletic teams. I want to ground each reader in these sports team values because I will merge them into traditional business values later in the book. It is primarily the deep-rooted differences in these two cultures that caused me to devote an entire chapter to conflict resolution techniques.

In my experience, it is precisely the failure to harmonize these two value systems in business — with their inherent conflict potential — that has caused many team building efforts to fail.

The biggest single barrier to building high-performance teams in corporations is a long-established cultural mindset and value system which subtly resists the formation of the true team spirit, which *must* exist before effective teams can be formed.

This book contains the observations and recommendations distilled from four decades of what I have read, heard, seen, and personally experienced with a variety of teams. We will ground ourselves in team terms and concepts, develop an understanding of the traditional values, and learn how to replace them with a team culture; I will also share some of the proven techniques for building teams and dealing with conflict, which I have used in building successful teams in several different organizations.

A Personal Experience

In order to set this book in the proper context, I want to share a personal team building experience that brought into dramatic focus all the team values, elements, characteristics, and skills to produce incredible results under the most adverse of conditions – a combat flying squadron in war time. As the tale unfolds, please remember that similar results are possible with teams in business, government, or even non-profit volunteer organizations. The secret is teamwork which has universal application.

The story I am about to relate will probably make you say, "OOPS, Pete has just breached credibility. I simply do not believe the numbers you have offered; there must be a typographical error!" Well, the story is true; the facts can be verified in the official record of combat missions flown by the 20th Tactical Air Support Squadron (TASS) at DaNang Air Base, Vietnam during the period June 1971 – May 1972. I was the Air Operations Officer and was proud to be a part of a combat unit that underwent the remarkable transformation from an average flying squadron with average performance to a focused team that achieved remarkable combat records, never seen before or since.

The Background

The North Vietnamese Army's mission was to move tons of war materiel (guns, bullets, rockets, fuel, food, etc.) from North Vietnam south through the jungles of Laos into South Vietnam to resupply their troops and the Viet Cong, in their effort to defeat the government of South Vietnam. The massive network of roads, bridges, tunnels, and anti-aircraft guns in Laos became known as the Ho Chi Minh Trail.

The mission of the 20th TASS was to fly daylight visual reconnaissance missions over assigned geographical sectors of "the Trail" to detect the movement of camouflaged trucks (large green bushes moving through the jungle), then mark those targets with white phosphorous smoke rockets and direct fighter bombers to destroy the trucks and war materiels; this game of hide, seek, and destroy is called interdiction.

The pilots of the 20th TASS were called forward air controllers (FACs). A typical day at the office was five hours of an angry slugfest in which we dropped bombs on them and they shot flak at us. Some days we won; other days they did.

Every organization has *measures of merit*: in sports it is the championship; in business it is profits; in education it is enlightened students; in combat, for us, it was sorties (missions) flown and trucks destroyed.

One measure of merit for the 20th TASS was the number of consecutive missions flown without a mission failure (which means failure to launch a scheduled mission). Prior to my arrival, the longest number of missions flown consecutively was 27. When the unit reached 27, they failed to fly an assigned mission, and they had to go back to zero and start over. The group commander assigned me to the 20th TASS. My main task, he charged, was to try to help to rebuild the organization. In fact, I was advised they had had more airplane losses from accidents and pilot error than from shoot downs from the enemy; it was a marginal unit, at best.

The Obvious Problem

When I arrived on the scene, it became relatively obvious that the problems of the organization had to do with leadership, training, motivation, a lack of teamwork, and a generally poor consistency of effort. After becoming combat mission ready, I assessed the situation and designed a radically different structure and process for using our resources for the assigned task, which was to fly combat missions during daylight hours over the Trail. If we did not fly, the enemy trucks rolled south toward their destination with impunity. Our OV-10 Broncos and O-2 Cessna Skymasters aircraft flew daytime missions, and the C-130 gunships covered the Trail at night. It was also evident that the units within the squadron—maintenance, personal equipment, intelligence, support systems, dining hall, the pilots, the operations personnel, the administrative staff, radio operators—were all part of the 20th TASS, but they did not perceive themselves as a single team contributing to a larger squadron effort. Maintenance had their own problems and concerns; the pilots had theirs; and the support people willingly blamed their problems on the maintenance personnel and the pilots. Rather than thinking of this as a larger unit—as one squadron with a single mission—those smaller sub-units tended to think of their own detailed function as their overall purpose. This was sub-optimization at its worst.

After discussing my ideas with my squadron commander, he agreed to allow me to fly to Saigon to 7th Air Force Headquarters to attempt to sell the concepts to our senior leaders. The approach was so different that any decision to implement such a plan was, as he put it, "well above my pay grade." I learned a valuable lesson during my two-day visit to 7th AF Headquarters: "Never ask permission from anyone who only has authority to say 'no'." I found that the Lt. Colonels, Colonels, and Brigadier Generals were not authorized to make such exceptions to policy.

The 30-Day Test

I finally briefed a Major General who held the "yes" card; he was empowered to make such a decision. He saw the value of the concept and gave us an opportunity: "I'll authorize a 30-day test. If we see no significant improvement in the overall operation of your squadron in one month, you will revert back to the way we have always scheduled combat missions here in Vietnam."

When I returned, the squadron commander called the key staff together. We started with some old-fashioned team building. We all had one single purpose, namely to get the bombs on target and everyone home alive. In order to improve internal communications, we started having a maintenance officer attend the operations meetings and an operations officer attended the maintenance meetings. We began to train, document, and hold supervisors accountable for the performance of their people. When someone did a particularly good job, we praised his supervisor. Conversely, when someone dropped the ball, his supervisor had to explain what happened and what exactly he was going to do to prevent recurrence.

We began to have complete squadron social functions, instead of the previously held "pilot parties," "maintenance beer busts," etc. We soon had erased the "we/they" lines of division and created a 20th TASS unit esprit de corps.

As we implemented the new scheduling concept, everyone knew the importance of an individual specific task to the overall goal, which was to fly successful missions! When minor glitches occurred, the objective was to fix the problem—not assign blame.

The Broken Record

Within a week, we broke the previous record of 27 consecutive missions flown. We placed the sign at the front gate with changeable numbers, so we could let the entire squadron know the tally every day. We were normally assigned 13-15 missions per day, so every day we succeeded, the tally jumped by that amount. When we hit 50, the squadron commander put a congratulatory letter on the bulletin board. When we hit 100, the commander of the 366 Tactical Fighter Wing (our parent unit) sent a letter of commendation. When we hit 200, we could see a visible transformation in everyone and everything about the 20th TASS; our squadron area was more attractive, our jeeps were cleaner, we all looked sharper, and we wore our 20th TASS ball caps and unit patches with great pride. The base newspaper began to write articles about our unit and its people.

When we hit 400, we began to receive staff visits from 7th Air Force Colonels to praise us and "see what the hell we were doing." When 800 went on the sign, General officers began to stop by; when 1000 was posted, we had one hell of a party! The total 1500 missions attracted the attention of the visiting Congressmen and associated news media.

How Many Missions?

Let's catch our breath a moment to study the anatomy of the remarkable team success. You could wake up any member of our unit—from the lowest-ranking airman to the commander—from a dead sleep and ask, "How many missions?" They could tell you precisely. Can you imagine how many times people rechecked their work to be sure they were not the person responsible for breaking this history-making chain of successful missions? We began to see true excellence at every level of the unit.

On the 154th day of consecutive missions flown, we had two FACs shot down at the same time. As expected, we diverted several aircraft to the search and rescue operation to recover the downed pilots from the enemy-infested jungle. We got them both out, thank God, but we broke the chain at 2124 missions.

The most amazing aspect of this story was this same unit had only flown 27 previous missions and was comprised of basically the same people, skills, aircraft, targets, weather, and facilities as the unit that flew over 2100 missions — the only major difference was teamwork.

This book will disclose all the tools and techniques that helped make this happen. I have seen these same concepts and skills work in many business organizations.

```
┌─────────────────────────────┐
│                             │
│        Chapter 1            │
│                             │
└─────────────────────────────┘
```

Team Terms and Concepts

The foundation of all understanding is a shared language. Before we can communicate ideas, we must first encode them in words, a color, a gesture, a sound. To express the idea of love, we say, "I love you." The color red is the universal color of an exit; the military salute is a gesture to indicate the idea of respect; and we all know what a flashing blue light behind us means. The process of communication is the exchanging of codes which represent or convey the ideas we hope to communicate.

Mankind has been studying leadership for centuries. By this time we should at least have a definition that enjoys wide acceptance. Research of the literature reveals over 130 definitions of leadership. I vote for the definition offered by Dr. Ken Blanchard, co-author of *The One Minute Manager*: "Leadership is the process of influencing the activities of an individual or a group in efforts toward goal achievement in a given situation."

Since leadership is one of the foundational elements of teamwork, it is not surprising that definitions of teams abound, also. Jon R. Katzenbach and Douglas K. Smith (*The Wisdom of Teams*) define a team as "A small number of people with complementary skills who are committed to a common purpose, approach, and performance goals for which they hold themselves mutually accountable." That is as fine a definition of teams as I have seen; it is brief but contains all the components upon which this book is built.

What constitutes a *small number* is debatable; however, that figure is driven by the number of discreet skills needed for a particular team to succeed. If ten skills are needed and five people have all those skills among themselves, then five team members is adequate. However, if the skills are complex and diverse, then you may need ten experts to comprise the correct *small number*.

The notion that the team members possess *complementary skills* creates the foundation for interdependence, which will be addressed in greater depth later. *Skills* should be differentiated from *knowledge*. Education is the transfer of concepts and principles: the output of education is knowledge. We demonstrate our knowledge by taking exams and discussing the concepts orally or in a written format.

Performance Is Skill-Based

In contrast, training is the transfer of skills. We demonstrate the skills we possess by actually *doing* a task. Please take special note of this statement: *Performance is skill-based, not knowledge-based.* The mere fact that a student pilot may understand aerodynamics, lift, drag, and Bernoulli's principle, and can make a perfect score on the final examination does not mean that the person will have the skills (ability) to land an airplane safely. One of the best definitions of training I heard many years ago was "to make proficient through instruction and practice in a climate of high self-esteem." Effective training develops skills, which help team members contribute to success. Hence, I agree with Katzenbach and Smith in stating that team members must have "complementary skills," because, as stated in the introduction, effective teams are known for what they *do*, not for what they talk about.

Commitment Is Important

Team members are committed to a common purpose, approach, and performance goals. The term *committed* is an absolute concept; there is no such thing as partially committed — you are either completely, totally, 100% committed or you are not! We'll discuss the idea of commitment in Chapters 3 and 4 as this concept relates to values. *Common purpose* is the goal, outcome, result, or objective that all team members share in their heart of hearts. They understand it; they own it; and they value it above their own personal needs, goals, or desires. In a word, the team's common purpose dwarfs even individual egos.

The team shares an approach to achieving a common purpose. This idea of shared approach has been the undoing of many teams; it is one of the toughest hurdles I have faced as a team building consultant. Teams that easily agree on "what" and "why" can self-destruct on the question of "how."

For some reason, people will cooperate and collaborate on developing a common purpose; some huge egos have willingly yielded to a worthy common purpose as well as the need for the diversity of complementary skills. But when they tackle the issue of a common approach, some people feel compelled to drive the team to their approach to the exclusion of all others. This shift in thinking is often so subtle they don't even know they are experiencing it. Many are so convinced that their approach is best that they can virtually destroy the team's emotional foundation in their blinding desire to help.

In a postmortem interview with a team member after a decision to abandon the team approach and revert to the traditional model—where the most senior person makes the decisions, he lamented, "I think teamwork is great, but those people simply would not listen to my approach. I have got a lot of experience in the subject, and I know what I am doing."

I learned from the other ex-team members that this person offered his approach and justified it because it had worked for him in the past. However, when other team members began to ask if improvements, adjustments, modifications, or other creative strategies would improve the process, he became defensive, argumentative, obstinate, and just plain obnoxious. He discounted the comments from other team members with "You don't know what in the hell you're talking about."

There Is No "I" in Team

In a subsequent counseling session, he could not understand how his behavior related to paradigms which cause psychological blocking of new and different ideas that may have conflicted with his perception of what was right. I was unable to help this man see the value of creative and critical thinking in *all* facets of team performance, particularly in the collaborative effort to define a common approach. We concluded our interview with his observation: "Pete, you don't know what in the hell you're talking about, either."

In a final attempt to help him understand himself, I had jotted down his remark verbatim. "I think team work is great, but those people simply would not listen to my approach. I've got a lot of experience in the subject, and I know what I'm doing!" I slipped my tablet across the table and asked him to underscore every personal reference of "I" or "my." After he marked five personal references, I said, "There is no 'I' in the spelling of TEAM."

"The Buck Stops Here"

The concluding phrase of the definition of a team ...*for which they hold themselves mutually accountable* is powerful. The dictionary defines mutual as "directed toward the other or the others...having the same feelings one for the other." This tends to bond the team emotionally together irrespective of the presence of a boss or supervisor. The team is emotionally anchored to each other, not to some authority figure.

Finally, "accountable" implies being answerable and responsible. As President Harry Truman put it, "The buck stops here..."

Two Kinds of Teams

Our analysis of teams requires a few more terms or building blocks for our understanding. There are two kinds of teams.

In *co-acting* teams, the members of the team work independently in that the success of one team member is *not* related to the efforts of any other team member. The classic co-acting team in business is the sales force; the success of the salesperson in New York is not affected by the efforts of the salesperson in Los Angeles. In co-acting organizations, the classic motivational strategy is competition. What gets the sales force out of the hotel or home and dealing with the rejection all salespersons face is the valued consequences of winning the sales contest — a trip, prize, bonus, or award. Motivation is determined, in large measure, by the valued, positive consequences people experience for making sales or the feared, negative consequences if they do not sell (i.e., termination, reprimand, or the humiliation of coming in at the bottom of the sales performance list). Now let us examine how co-acting team members communicate with one another.

The PULL System and PUSH System

There are two types of communication systems; one is a PULL system, in which information flows *upon demand*. The demand is a question or request.

For example, I need some information to accomplish a task. I think Barbara, my administrative assistant, has the information. I might ask (pull), "Barbara, what is the status of the Pennzoil project?" She tells me. All recurring reports are pull systems.

The other type of communication system is a PUSH system, in which information flows *without demand*. Barbara might become aware of some information she thinks would be of value to me, so she tells me or "pushes" it to me without my asking.

The great difference between pull and push systems is that pull systems meet the needs of the person pulling the information; push systems not only meet those same needs but they build positive relationships.

Let us assume that a co-worker of mine in the accounting department is on a jetliner. She browses through the airline magazines and notices an article on organizational development. She might think, "This article could be of value to Pete Land since he is a management consultant." She will clip out the article and send it to me with a note. "Pete, I saw this article on a recent flight; thought you might appreciate it."

What is my reaction when I receive this information that my colleague "pushed" to me? I not only gain from reading an article in my field, but I also have a very positive feeling about my colleague who was thoughful enough to (1) know enough about me and my business to realize what was of value to me and (2) take the time and trouble to send or "push" it to me. (3) I sense her primary motivation for doing so was to help me win.

You may rest assured that I will be sensitive to

articles on accounting and will "push" valued information to her. One note of caution: push information only works when you know enough about the other party to know what information has high value and which information might be viewed as junk mail by the recipient.

Bottom line—in order for push systems to truly build positive relationships, there must be sufficient understanding about your colleague's business to know what information is important to the individual.

Now, let us return to how co-acting team members tend to communicate when the motivational strategy is competition. If the salesperson in New York learns an effective technique which results in a sale, he or she now has moved closer to winning the sales award or contest. Do you think this person is going to call the salesperson in Los Angeles and push this information (new technique) to them? Don't bet on it!

You can also expect the Los Angeles salesperson to "close-hold" any skills and techniques he or she may develop. And, so it is with co-acting, independent team players.

The Interacting Team

The only other kind of team in captivity is an *interacting* team, in which the members of the team work *inter*dependently. We will know they are interacting if the success of one member is related to the efforts of other team members. Better yet, the success of the entire team is dependent upon the efforts of *all* team members.

The classic example of an interacting team is a sports team, such as a football team. A quarterback cannot score a touchdown acting alone. Touchdowns are made when the players in every position cooperate and collaborate both in the huddle and at the snap of the ball. You will also notice that the entire team goes to the victory banquet, not just the quarterback.

Interacting teams should always have group reward systems which honor the group's collective effort. In business, the manufacturing team's cooperation is vital to successfully making the product. The outputs of the engineering department (drawings) become the required inputs for the production department, which sends their output (the product) to the shipping department.

Competition Among Team Members Is Dysfunctional

The key difference between co-acting and interacting teams is that in an interacting setting, competition among and between team members is totally dysfunctional. It simply makes no sense for people to compete when they are all wearing the same color uniform and are in the same company.

One would think that mature business organizations would intuitively know that competition around the conference table at a staff meeting is inappropriate and draws attention and energy away from those factors that make the company competitive in the market place. We will shed more light on this negative phenomenon as we discuss the transition from traditional to team values in Chapter 4.

Another term we should work thoroughly into daily vocabulary is "teammate." You might consider "team member" and "teammate" to be synonymous. I have detected a subtle difference through my extensive study of scores of teams over the years.

The image conjured up by the word "team member" has many positive aspects, but while membership implies belonging to a certain group, such as "member of a particular church/synagogue" or "member of a political party," it falls short in addressing the relationship between the members. As a member of a large church, I have the option to attend and participate, or not. There are fellow church members I have never met. Despite my level of involvement and my relationship with other members, I am still a member.

Shift from "Member" to "Mate"

In contrast, when I observe very mature and effective teams, they often refer to the people on their team as "teammates." The word "mate" seems to encompass a genuine relationship of closeness, caring, and mutual respect that is not always found in teams who refer to each other as "members." Most mature teams do not formally decide to shift from "member" to "mate," but it is a joy to see this happen naturally as the teams mature.

In discussing this shift with a person on a mature team, he said: "When we started to build this team several months ago, I really liked and respected the team members. But, today I can honestly say I actually love my teammates." You now understand why "teammates" will be used generously in this book.

As the final draft of this book took shape, I asked a long-time colleague, Gail Kelley-Webb, to review it. Gail is President of St. Charles Consulting in Luling, Louisiana, and is an expert at building high performance teams. One reason for her success is that she addresses all the traditional team building dimensions but takes it to the next level of what she calls "attunement."

Attunement

"Alignment" is widely understood to be a sharing of goals, objectives — yes, even values. However, Gail's concept of "attunement" means that the teammates also share a spirit of trust, ambition, caring, support and an unflinching belief in each other. She and I have both found, in altogether different settings, that it is the "intangible feelings" that distinguish truly world-class teams. It is this shared spirit that helps teams rebound from setbacks and adversity. There exists a *spiritual buoyancy* that allows teammates to focus on lessons learned rather than disappointment when problems occur. I am constantly reminding my clients that "The mistakes we make are *temporary;* the lessons they teach us are *permanent.*"

There is a healing effect when teammates look trouble squarely in the eye and say confidently, "There is simply *no* problem that our team cannot solve when we work together." These thoughts of complete trust and reinforcing confidence leave no time or energy for feelings of resentment or despair.

Remember to Say "Yet"

When I was a green Air Force Lieutenant, my boss, a senior colonel with lots of gray hair and ribbons on his chest, assigned me an area of responsibility. Colonel Dutch Lammert was one of the best leaders I have ever known. When he assigned me a duty in which I had absolutely no experience and very little knowledge, I protested, "Colonel, I am reluctant to accept these duties because I have no experience and almost no knowledge of this subject."

I have long remembered his sage reply: "Pete, a lack of knowledge is a *temporary* condition. You can resolve that problem rapidly by intense study. I will provide my counsel to help develop your *experience*, but I expect you to gain the *knowledge* quickly." He asked me to repeat the statement: "I don't know anything about this subject," and then he said, "Add the word 'yet' to your sentence." The result is a powerful statement: "I don't know anything about this subject, yet!"

The concept of "yet" means we are always under construction; learning every day. Experience is gained over time—every iteration, every cycle, every attempt to perform helps build our core of experience. Colonel Lammert reminded me that the process of gaining experience is much less painful if we begin with an in-depth study, garner as much knowledge as possible, and then actually begin to perform the task.

On occasion, I have been approached by a troubled manager who is bemoaning the fact that a particular supervisor "simply *cannot* conduct an effective performance appraisal." Without the word "yet," that statement often becomes a self-fulfilling prophecy because the manager assumes the person cannot do the task, so he discontinues all training activities to develop those skills.

However, when I ask the manager to say "yet," the entire situation shifts to "work in progress," the training continues, and, to no one's surprise, the supervisor becomes competent at conducting performance appraisals.

Many thanks to Colonel Dutch Lammert, my boss in Germany in 1962, for reminding us that "yet" is a powerful word.

Chapter 2

Traditional Organizational Values

========

The roots of our present traditional organizational values began with the Industrial Revolution. Prior to the advent of the Industrial Age, we were mainly an agrarian society. Many of our citizens lived and worked on farms; agriculture dominated the lives of many Americans around the turn of the century. The average family could, literally, carve a life out of the wilderness. They cut down the trees to build a house, cleared the stumps, and planted and harvested crops to feed the family and to sell for cash.

Our history is replete with examples of rugged individuals who succeeded by the sweat of the brow. It is not difficult to understand why Americans tend to honor individual achievement. In the city squares of our towns, you will see a pedestal with a statue of one famous person, not of a group. Even in professional sports today, superstars and free agents often make eight to ten times the salary of some of their fellow teammates. And, so it is in corporate America. The outstanding salesperson or the strongest individual contributor receives the huge compensation package and, often, outrageous bonuses.

In our culture today, everyone wants to win. We understand General Douglas MacArthur's admonition, "There is no substitute for victory," since in war, being runner-up is unacceptable. We honor such sports legends as Vince Lombardi, who said repeatedly, "Winning is not everything; it's the only thing." Our entire system of justice is driven by winning a case or judgment. The very nature of the free enterprise business system is competition with its array of winners and losers. Our political system produces winners and losers after every election.

As we discussed in Chapter 1, in co-acting teams, the members work independently, like a sales force. When the success of one salesperson is not related to or affected by another salesperson, we create a contest for the top salesperson, which is, once again, a competitive system producing one winner and lots of losers.

Our entire educational system fosters co-acting behavior with grades and class standing being the rewards for individual achievement. We are simply expected to do our own work. Diplomas and degrees are presented to individuals for individual, personal, and co-acting performance.

While there are many benefits from a system that creates personal accountability, this deeply-seated cultural value tends to work in opposition to a true system of interdependence (interacting teams). Bottom line—co-acting and interacting values tend to be mutually exclusive; i.e., they cannot exist at the same place at the same time for the same two groups.

It is ironic that employees spend their entire formative years in schools where co-acting behavior is honored only to join an organization upon graduation where interacting behavior is necessary to the team's (company's) success in a harshly competitive business environment.

Keep Ego in Perspective

Add to this concept the deeply-rooted cultural bias: "Work hard, do your best, and you will succeed" (which is the traditional way we compensate and reward hard work); then the problem becomes more complex. Many companies have individual goals by which employees are evaluated at year-end. If they make their performance objectives (budget, sales, goals, etc.), they may get a sizable raise or bonus.

I recall in Psychology 101 the professor stating, "You tend to get what you honor and reinforce." As an American, I am guilty as charged! I love standing for praise and recognition; who doesn't? But I'm beginning to understand the comment of a Japanese businessman during one of my consulting engagements with a Japanese firm. He said, only partly in jest, "Most Americans have egos bigger than Nebraska." However, it is refreshing to see a genuine high performer who has his/her ego in perspective. That is a true sign of greatness.

Unfortunately, I have interviewed hundreds of

executives, managers, and supervisors during team-building activities, and I have never met one who, when push came to shove, would not skim off just a little extra credit to be sure he/she looked good. Deep under the surface platitudes and team talk, there lurks a hard core of enlightened self-interest that very few would admit to in public.

There is no such thing as meaningless behavior. If the average corporate team player talks a good teamwork game, but subtly looks out for number one, there are perfectly valid reasons why the person does so. One simply cannot suppress the American desire to win. Before we can successfully build a mature team in an American business, we must understand why there exists this small, yet important, kernel of reluctance.

This single issue is at the very heart of team building. It is often the root cause for a team's failure, but it is so obscure that the team members themselves often do not recognize it. When this last particle of reserved self-interest falls, then the team members become teammates. Only then does the team possess the potential for true greatness.

Surrender the "Me" to the "We"

In the national best seller, *Sacred Hoops* by Phil Jackson and Hugh Delehanty, Coach Jackson describes some of the challenges of having Michael Jordan on the Chicago Bulls' professional basketball team. During his first years with the team, he had to be cajoled into making sacrifices for the team and share the spotlight. But as Jordan matured, Jackson writes, "Now he was an older, wiser player who understood that it wasn't brilliant individual performances that made great teams but the energy that is unleashed when players put their ego aside and work toward a common goal. Good teams become great ones when the members trust each other enough to surrender the 'me' for the 'we'."

This idea is equally as important in corporate America today.

Chapter 3

Team Values, Elements, And Characteristics

Think of an effective team as the glorious output of many unglamorous but important inputs. We should not focus on the outputs because they will occur if the correct inputs are provided in the proper mix and at the appropriate time. Imagine that team building is analogous to making a cake. To make a delicious cake (effective team), we refer to a proven recipe that, when followed meticulously, has produced a delectable cake for dessert. However, how tasty is the cake if you leave out the flour or cook it for half the time specified in the recipe?

Remember the cake when you begin to assemble and mix the ingredients for producing an effective team. The first ingredient is a set of *TEAM VALUES* that must be taught, understood, modeled, and REWARDED by everyone on the team.

Team Values

1. THE GOAL OF OUR TEAM IS MORE IMPORTANT THAN ANYTHING WE CAN ACCOMPLISH INDIVIDUALLY. Everyone must fully appreciate that the goal of the team is worthy of a coordinated, interactive team effort. Additionally, everyone must know that any co-acting behavior, which creates internal conflict, will put the overall team goals at risk.

2. ACHIEVING THE TEAM GOAL WILL CREATE FAR MORE BENEFITS AND REWARDS FOR EVERYONE WHO PARTICIPATES IN THE TEAM ACTIVITY THAN FOR ANY SINGLE PERSON ACTING INDIVIDUALLY. One side benefit of this mindset is that only those teammates who unselfishly dedicate themselves to true interacting behavior can personally accept the psychological rewards of high self-esteem for their team's achieving its goal. Only when every teammate personally values the intrinsic rewards for the team's success will he/she then give up the psychological rewards (personal glory) for drawing individual attention.

3. INTERACTING BEHAVIOR MUST BE THE NORM. Everyone must know and fully appreciate the value of his/her particular contribution as well as the importance of everyone else's contribution. This is where positive feedback is appropriate.

4. ANY CO-ACTING BEHAVIOR MUST BE DISHONORED BY THE TEAM. Not only should the team reject such behavior, but it should also openly condemn "grand-

standing." Corrective feedback is the appropriate tool here. Both corrective and positive feedback skills will be developed completely in Chapter 4.

Team Elements

Team elements are different from values. Values tend to be subjective and intangible, whereas elements are more objective and tangible. The literature suggests the following:

Charter

The charter is the team's overall reason for being. It is similar to a mission or vision statement. The charter does not normally change over time, whereas many strategies and/or goals can be accomplished to support the team's charter. Visualize the charter as the sign out in front of the company. The goals are the posts holding up the sign (charter).

Steelcase, Inc., based in Grand Rapids, Michigan, is one of the most successful manufacturers of office furniture in the world. Several years ago, it was selected as one of the top 100 companies in America. In my consulting relationship with Steelcase, I learned one of their secrets to success—everyone knows the charter.

If you were to wake up two Steelcase employees, e.g., the CEO and one of the truck drivers, from a deep sleep and ask the question: "What is your charter?"you would get the same answer from both people: "We deliver quality products on time." If you were to further ask the CEO and truck driver,

"What do you do to contribute to delivering quality products on time?" you would, of course, get totally different responses.

At Steelcase, as well as at other successful organizations, there are many different job descriptions, but they all focus on one charter: "We deliver quality products on time." Please note that they start their charter with the collective pronoun "we." You will never see the words "I," "me," "my," or "they" in any charter. It's always "we," "us," "our!"

Interdependence

Interdependence must become part of the team culture. Everyone should be able to recognize co-acting and interacting behavior. Co-acting behavior should be rejected, and interacting behavior should be rewarded. Everyone must understand pull and push communications. Each should learn enough about the other functions in the team to be able to push valued information to help the other teammates win.

I learned the importance of interdependence during a recent team building engagement with a Fortune 500 manufacturing company. The CEO contacted me because he perceived there was negative conflict between department heads, which was damaging the company's productivity and profits.

In one of the team building exercises, I had each of the department heads meet with the managers/supervisors in their department. Their task was to list what positive inputs/contributions each of the other departments made to theirs. For example, the engineering department staff would list all positive inputs to engineering from administration, sales, marketing, production, etc.

The larger group reassembled to share their lists with the other departments. Each department head, in turn, told the other departments what they appreciated. You can well imagine that this was a very positive experience for everyone. We were building positive confrontation credits.

Phase Two of the exercise was to return to their smaller groups and list everything they would like to see *more of* or *less of* from the other departments. We insisted that they list specific activities which could be measured. For example, instead of requesting, "Be more responsive to our needs," we got such comments as, "We need two copies of the production report by noon on the fifth working day of the month." (In the past, they were only getting one copy on the eighth day).

As groups reassembled, each department would state specific needs and concerns. We actually "contracted" to comply, if at all possible. If a request could not be honored, then the reason was explained and a compromise was negotiated. We met again 30 days later to follow up; the result was very positive.

This process builds the value and importance of interdependence; we all learned that we need each other to succeed as a greater whole. (Review Appendix D).

Accountability

Accountability for the team performance is internalized by everyone. In team building workshops, I often pose these two questions to the team. "In one year from today, if this team is truly succeeding by every measure of merit (profits, quality, high morale, low turnover, etc.), whose *fault* is it?" They will smile and say in unison "Ours" or "Mine." I confirm that "Yes, your team will be praised for all your successes; you would fairly accept full accountability for the glory."

I continue, "However, if a year from now this team is a total disaster—profits and quality are abominable, morale is low, and turnover is high, whose *fault* is that?" There is usually an uncomfortable silence. The team members sneak a glimpse at who they think will be the weak link and bring the team crashing down. Then, one of the more courageous members will say, "It will be *our* fault; we all must say 'my fault!'"

It is easy to accept credit, but it takes a team with true character to accept the joint and personal accountability for the failures. When they can all say truthfully that "Any failure is *my* fault," then true accountability has been created.

These concepts of clear charter, interdependence, and accountability were clearly exemplified by a legendary event which occurred during the 1992 Summer Olympics in Barcelona, Spain.

The Dream Team

Scores of nations put their best basketball players on a national team, practiced for months, and sent them to Barcelona in hopes of winning the gold medal; the USA did the same. We skimmed the cream from the top of the NBA and assembled such notables as Michael Jordan, Charles Barkley, Magic

Johnson, Scottie Pippen, et al. and created what the pundits quickly labeled "The Dream Team."

Without a doubt, these men were America's best basketball players with incomes and, in some cases, egos to match. Bear in mind that throughout the professional basketball season, these men were primarily on different teams whose success was measured on how frequently and how completely they defeated the other team. In fact, many of the Dream Team members were arch rivals; if their team won, then the other team had to taste the agony of defeat.

I have met a few professional athletes in several different sports, but they all share two values: (1) they love to win; (2) they hate to lose.

Because of these intense feelings borne out of years of competition, some sports writers predicted that this small group of millionaires would not and could not gel as a true team and perform effectively; some predicted they would be defeated by a team of lesser skill but greater teamwork.

The entire world watched and wondered — could these very talented athletes park their egos at courtside? Their egos had been nourished by celebrity product endorsements, the frenzied adulation of millions of fans, pictures on billboards, and huge salaries. And now there was the temptation of the Olympics, with the largest audience in the world watching and replaying their every move.

Winning the Gold

At the first tip-off, the world witnessed an incredible transformation of team values. The players completely forgot about the Chicago Bulls, the LA Lakers, or the Phoenix Suns. Every teammate focused on one goal, one purpose, one reason for being: to win the gold for the USA.

In the lightning-fast game of basketball, the players make thousands of decisions—pass, shoot, fake, run, stop; many choices are made in a millisecond and the outcome of the game hangs in the balance. If the ball is passed to Jordan, he has only a split second to decide to shoot or pass. There is no time to factor values into the equation; he must act instinctively. But the instinctive actions are driven by a predetermined set of beliefs and values that allows him to act effectively within a brief window of opportunity— win the gold for the USA.

As the world recalls, and the record books reflect, in the seven games the Dream Team played against the best teams the world could field, they scored an amazing 938 points, averaging 117.3 points per game. They defeated their opponents by an average margin of 43.8 points. Some observers felt they limited the score to keep from humiliating another nation's best team. Is there any doubt that with their egos parked at courtside the Dream *TEAM* handily won the gold for the USA?

"Bake a Team"

It is evident to me that the Dream Team's incredible success was driven, in large measure, by the fact that they had personally internalized the values of the team's goal, which could only be achieved by performing as an interacting team. I am not persuaded that these men met to discuss formally the concepts we have introduced here; but they have learned, through years of successful athletic competition, what many business leaders have yet to understand. Competition is only appropriate vis-à-vis the opposing team or company. We should *never* compete within our own organization.

Cooperation/collaboration must be the order of the day within the "family" if we are to bring the full potential of our team to address the competitive pressures of business. The teams (companies) who cooperate/collaborate with their colleagues invariably "win the gold" for their organizations.

So, there you have the three major elements needed to "bake" a team—(1) a charter, (2) interdependence, and (3) accountability.

Team Characteristics

Now that we have discussed values and elements, we should conclude this chapter with a description of team characteristics, which the dictionary defines as "distinguishing features or attributes." The team literature abounds with descriptors which characterize teams. Every author has personal thoughts on the subject; there is very little agreement. In light of the general state of flux in team building folklore, I will offer the four characteristics which make sense to me.

Intact Work Group

First, a team is an *intact work group*. I see a true team as a group of people who may or may not work in the same geographical area; they interact in person, by phone, teleconference, and/or by fax or e-mail on a regular basis. The group has an accepted membership, which may be formal or informal. If asked, they could list the names of the teammates; they would generally agree on who is *not* a member of their work group or team.

I have observed quite often in organizations with a strong hierarchical structure (chain of command) that the boss or supervisor is *not* considered to be a member of the team by the rank-and-file members. When a "boss" leans heavily on position power, then one of the negative consequences is that the group mentally excludes that person from their perception of their "intact work groups." When formal leaders (bosses) are excluded from the concept of the group, there tends to be a leadership void at the working level, which, unfortunately, may be filled by a strong informal leader who may or *may not* share the best overall mission of the group.

On rare occasions I have witnessed an unsettling rift between the boss and the workers. This situation is particularly stressful when the boss is legally accountable for the performance of the group and the informal leader is not. If the informal leader is so inclined, he or she can generate all manner of mischief for which the boss must take the blame.

Relative Permanence

The second characteristic is that the team is *relatively permanent* — it has a past, present, and future. The Green Bay Packers has been a professional football team for many seasons; I expect that the Packers will be around for many more years. Granted, the names on the roster change somewhat every season, but we can expect the Green Bay Packers, as a team, to be "packing" football stadiums for years to come.

For this same reason, we do not refer to the group that comes together to plan this year's Christmas Party as a team. It's an ad hoc committee and will cease to exist after the party is over and the bills are paid. Such a committee is temporary, not permanent.

A Group with a Leader

The third characteristic is that a team is normally a *group of peers with a leader;* there is always someone who provides that all-important focus of leadership. That is why in our discussion of *intact work groups* there should be one primary focus of leadership around which the entire team can coalesce. A boss and a different informal leader can play havoc with the focus of leadership.

You have noticed that when a company has been the victim of a hostile takeover, the key leaders in the acquired company are often outplaced (fired). It is simply easier to change the culture of the acquired company by creating an instant leadership void and then filling that void with someone who reflects the values and views of the new owner. The key leaders in the acquired company were loyal to the previous values and, therefore, may have difficulty accepting the new culture.

We Are Unique

The final characteristic is that most teams see themselves as unique or in a *special situation.* In my years of consulting, I have heard this phrase hundreds of times, "We are unique." That statement is not only popular, but it is also true. Every person is different; we have our strengths and weaknesses. We are all flawed.

However, for some inexplicable reason, when we assemble a group of imperfect people into an organization, we expect it to be perfect. We have trouble accepting that imperfect people do not make perfect organizations.

The uniqueness of each organization comes from the continuous interaction of the ever-changing strengths and weaknesses of each individual member. Each of us is developing our skills daily, and we constantly confront situations which surface weaknesses that we need to strengthen.

The phrase "we are unique" is correct when a member of that team reflects on the blend of personalities, challenges, strengths, and weaknesses of that group. Each member sees his/her team at a level of specificity that acknowledges the fact that "There is no other group in the world exactly like ours today. We also know that tomorrow the team will be slightly different."

It is safe to say that in organizations, nothing is static; many things change frequently. Failure to consider this particular characteristic, *unique or special situations*, and attendant dynamics has been, in my experience, the downfall of many otherwise well-designed team building strategies. I will discuss how to deal with this all-important characteristic as we study the special team building assessment strategies in Chapter 6.

Summary

We have presented the building blocks of values, elements, and characteristics, which combine to make a solid team. Team **values** are as follows: (1) the team goal is more important than any individual goals; (2) achieving the team goal creates more benefits for everyone than any one person can create acting individually; (3) interacting behavior must be the norm; (4) co-acting behavior must be unacceptable to the team.

Team **elements** are as follows: (1) a clear charter, (2) interdependence, and (3) accountability. And, the following **characteristics** are foundational to the team: (1) intact work groups, (2) relative permanence, (3) group of peers with a leader, and (4) appreciation for the uniqueness of the team's special situation.

Chapter 4

The Transition from Traditional to Team Values

I heard years ago that Decisions lead to Activities and Activities produce Results. We know that Results are the outcome of Activities, not Decisions and that Activities are *skill-based*, not knowledge-based. A successful carpenter has the tools he needs (hammer and nails), the knowledge (he knows when a hammer and nail are appropriate in a building situation), and, most importantly, he has the *skills* to use the tools. He routinely drives nails and builds structures of lasting usefulness and beauty.

I, too, have the tools (hammer and nails), and I know when I should use hammer and nails in a building situation. But, I invariably hit my thumb and bend the nails. I lack one critical element, which the carpenter possesses—the *skills* to use the tools.

Knowledge and tools are of little value until they are blended with the necessary skills to create something of value.

This concept applies to team building. If we are not enjoying the marvelous fruits of interactive teamwork and are plagued with apathetic employees, then we simply need to accept the reality that the past and present activities in which we have participated have produced our present undesirable result. We will continue to get the *same* result as long as we perform the *same* activity.

However, if we want a new result (true team players), then we simply have no choice other than to involve ourselves in a different set of activities (team building and coaching). We have no choice but to learn and practice different skill-based activities.

Discard Old Habits

It is my intent in this chapter to move your frame of reference away from what may have been successful in the past. I want you to personally devalue some of your former ways of leading. Many of your skills have been effective and may continue to serve you well in the future.

However, autocratic styles are losing their effectiveness rapidly. Today and in the future, the "do it because I said so" style results in a down side that we can ill afford to experience. When you discard some old habit patterns, then the void created can be filled by a new and more productive value system, which will lead to successful management.

Traditionally, the focus of leadership was important; teams look toward a concept of **Shared Leader-**

ship. When teams are "doing their thing," there is always a focus of leadership — a quarterback, a team captain, a coach. One of the vulnerabilities of teams is that the leadership role tends to be focused on one person. If that person is absent, incapacitated, or otherwise not available, the team's effectiveness tends to lag. Coach Paul "Bear" Bryant, the winningest football coach among the major colleges, recognized this problem and stated, "I want a lot of leaders; then I'll build to them."

In *Managing to Get the Job Done*, I introduced the reader to the Pee Wee Vikings, the little league football team my eight-year-old son Steve (in the early 1970s) played on in Mt. Pleasant, South Carolina. As one of the coaches, I was asked to use proven team-building techniques to help the Vikings climb from their last-place position in the previous season. The book explains how the Vikings team became the uncontested champion of the Pee Wee league the very next season.

When we were coaching the Pee Wee Vikings, we applied Coach Bryant's leadership building concept as well. Before every game, the teams took the field for warm-up drills and calisthenics. Each of the two teams usually took half of the field and could see the opposing team's warm-up activities.

When the Vikings took the field, they formed a perfect circle for exercises. One player was designated as the leader and would be in the center of the circle. He would lead a four-count exercise and on the fourth count the entire team would count the repetitions: "One two three, *ONE*; one, two three, *TWO*; one, two, three *THREE*, etc. After ten repetitions, the leader would point to any other player, perhaps the least skilled player, to become the leader for the next exercise. Every player had an opportunity to assume a leadership role.

We drilled and practiced the warm-up routine just as if it were a touchdown play. Our players looked like a professional football team, particularly when compared to the team on the other end of the field. Other coaches told us later that the Vikings' warm-up session was very intimidating to our opposition. The greatest benefit was that we were never without leadership on the field, regardless of who was playing.

Teams tend to be internally motivated rather than externally driven. They have a value to **keep everyone on mental tiptoes**.

As teams form, become effective, and win, there is a natural tendency to relax and rest on their laurels. It is human nature to want to pause long enough to bask in the spotlight while standing on a platform of success. Unfortunately, while this temporary coasting is pleasant, it works against those activities which gained the team success in the first place.

If we study teams closely, we notice an undulating cycle of success followed by a slowdown. The slowdown causes them to slip from the top, which motivates the team to the next successful effort, and the cycle repeats itself.

How does one deal with this almost inevitable human phenomenon? With the Pee Wee Vikings, the following technique worked extremely well; hopefully, you can adapt the concept to your team situation. After a convincing victory on Saturday, we all congratulated every player on the team for his contribution to the victory.

Every member of the team played in every game; there was never a clean uniform on our team at the end of any game. We told everyone to "be ready to contribute to the victory."

Hustle Like a Winner

After the game on Saturday, the boy who played running back and had made three touchdowns may reasonably assume he had earned that starting position for next Saturday's game. NOT SO!

When practice began the next Monday afternoon, every position on the team was open. Every player could try out for any position. If the star quarterback did not demonstrate and develop his skills during the entire week of practice, he would probably not make the starting team.

In a word, yesterday's laurels did not guarantee tomorrow's successes; only hard work and discipline all week earned a starting position for the next game.

It was most interesting as the young boys found out that the coaches really meant what they said. When one of the best players sat on the bench for the first half of an important game because he failed to "hustle like a winner" in practice, our team truly developed a "continuous improvement" value system.

What we meant by "hustle like a winner" was far more than their conduct on the practice field. Winners keep their school grades up, they eat properly, and get adequate rest. They arrive at practice on time, with their gear in good condition. They study the football rules and learn how to keep from drawing penalties.

Winners willingly do what is asked without complaining. True winners make a sincere effort to help their team members in any way they can. We learned later that a few of the players who made good grades in school were tutoring some of their teammates who were having problems with academics.

It was heart warming to learn that as the season progressed, groups of Pee Wee Vikings — rich and poor, black and white — were going to movies and socializing off the field as good friends. (They often wore their Viking jerseys.)

One of the rules that the coaches instituted was that no teammate could ever criticize a fellow teammate for any reason. If a player fumbled the ball or missed a tackle, his teammates never mentioned the mistake. As coaches we would ask, "Jimmy, what could you have done differently that would have helped you make that tackle?" He not only told the coaches, but his teammates learned that lesson, also.

You would be amazed at the bonding and mutual support that can develop when your teammates only help — never hurt. The last few pages may create images of a small group of young boys playing football. How, you may ask, does this Viking winning culture translate into the rough and tumble world of business with tight margins and unforgiving stockholders?

First, let me clear the air about margins and stockholders. I have never seen a stockholder who was unhappy about the company excelling by every measure of merit.

Football teams can win every game, and companies can set new benchmarks of excellence for their industry. Tight margins do not threaten companies that make huge profits.

When Vince Lombardi coached the Green Bay Packers to a Super Bowl Championship, his credo was to "Do the fundamentals perfectly." You may find it hard to believe, but the Pee Wee Vikings never stressed what they had to do to keep from losing; they only focused on what it would take to win.

State the Positive

It all boils down to a basic mindset about your team and how you visualize the future. The seeds of a healthy mindset are grounded in a totally positive and success-oriented culture. For example, coaches could admonish, "Don't fumble the ball!" Looking closely, you will notice that the word "don't" is loading a negative mindset; "fumble" is more of the same. With a steady diet of "don't fumble, don't miss the tackle, don't drop the pass," the mind tends to visualize such mistakes.

The Pee Wee Vikings were never fed negative thoughts. "Don't fumble" was replaced with "protect the football"; "don't miss the tackle" became "keep your head in front of the runner and keep your back straight as you *make* the tackle." "Don't drop the pass" took the positive tone of "look for the threads on the ball until it's locked in your arms."

Could the supervisor who snaps: "Don't be late to work" just as easily say: "The team needs you and your skills at 8:00 a.m."? Could the boss who harps on rejects and callbacks just as easily praise the improvements in quality and share letters of praise from enthusiastic customers?

As I consult with healthy companies built on effective teamwork, I have found one value they all share. The emphasis is on quality, continuous process improvement, legendary customer service, and the skills it takes to deliver these services. They have learned true success comes more from consistently doing positive acts than from attempting to reduce errors. Note once again these two more negatively loaded words — reduce errors.

One skill all successful teams possess is the ability for team members to give high impact positive feedback, plus corrective feedback, when necessary, given in a positive manner. Let's review how you do both.

In my first book, *Managing to Get the Job Done*, I discussed how to give positive feedback; if you've read that book, this will be a review. However, corrective feedback skills were not covered in that book. But, the key point to remember is that positive and corrective feedback is absolutely essential to a healthy team spirit. Feedback can be given by formal leaders, informal leaders, coaches or even other teammates.

Teams Thrive on Feedback

Coaches and Teammates Give Feedback

One thing I've noticed about most successful leaders is that they give high-impact feedback. Most leaders have a vision; they see the organization as it could be, not only as it is today. If the vision is to guide and motivate people, they must be able to see it. The role of a leader is to let people know how their present performance relates to the vision. That is called feedback.

When I see the Readiness x Willingness x Ability = Performance formula for success, I see feedback as the drawstring that ties all the elements together.

One of the most important responsibilities of leadership is to provide feedback to subordinates. As we know, people do not do jobs; instead they do tasks. Therefore, feedback must be given at the *task* level.

Figure 4-1

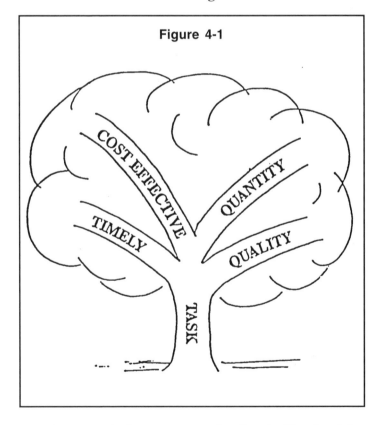

Figure 4-1 helps in giving feedback. Think of the job as the forest; the tasks are the trees and the various dimensions of the task are branches on the trees.

Every task has a qualitative dimension (it should be done correctly), a quantitative dimension (someone is always counting output), a timeliness dimension (early, on time, or late), and a cost-effective dimension (one should not use twenty sheets of letterhead to prepare one letter). The dimensions are actually the standards or expectations associated with each task. For feedback to be effective and of high impact to the subordinate, it should be related to the standards, whether expressed or implied, of these positive dimensions.

Let's assume I ask my administrative assistant, "Will you please type this letter for me? I need it for my ten a.m. meeting." I've asked her to accomplish one of the tasks that is a part of her job.

There's a qualitative dimension (it should be correct), a quantitative dimension (I want *one* letter and one to file), a timeliness dimension (I need it by ten), and a cost-effective dimension (use our expensive letterhead only for the final copy of the letter).

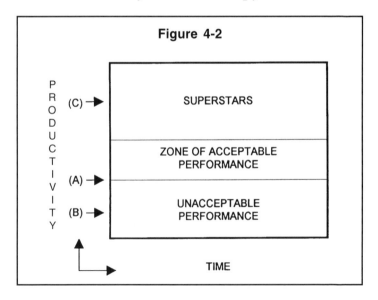

Figure 4-2

In *Figure 4-2*, the minimally acceptable level of performance (A) for the qualitative dimension is, in our example, no typos, proper format, and neatness. When we look at the qualitative dimension, (A) becomes two letters, one to mail and one for the file. The timeliness standard (A) is 10:00. Ten-thirty would represent a point below the minimally acceptable level (B). However, 8:30 is well above the standard, so we could rightfully see it at point (C) on the chart.

When we view the standard of cost effectiveness, (A) equals one piece of letterhead; using three would be at point (B) on the chart—wasteful. Let's now assume that my assistant placed a perfect letter on my desk at 8:30 that morning. If I value opportunities to provide positive reinforcement to her, I have an opportunity to praise her for meeting three of the task dimensions, but I'll get the greater impact by singling out the dimension she exceeded—timeliness.

Dr. Dick Leatherman, Chairman of International Training Consultants from Richmond, Virginia, has developed and marketed some of the finest training materials in the world. He offers the following first five steps to provide high-impact feedback. I have added steps six and seven.

Positive Feedback

1. Describe the positive situation, incident, behavior in detail. It is best to have first-hand knowledge and then to use first-person pronouns: I, me, my.

2. Tell the employee exactly why you value the action taken, i.e., saves time, money, or improves quality, etc.

3. Express your personal appreciation for the action.

4. Tell the employee you have confidence in his or her ability to do similar good work in the future.

5. Thank the person again, shake hands, or pat him or her on the back.

6. You may want to combine the doer and the deed — "That was an excellent piece of work; you are making a fine contribution to the company."

7. Positive feedback may be given in public or private, but public positive feedback is preferred.

I would say, "Thanks for completing this letter early. You gave me an opportunity to fine-tune it before the meeting. I appreciate your extra effort in this. If I ever need something done quickly, I know you're there to help. Thanks a lot."

The general output of such behavior on my part almost invariably produces the following response by my administrative assistant:

1. She feels her contribution to the mission is genuinely appreciated by her boss.

2. She is more inclined to do the same thing under similar conditions in the future.

3. She also knows that had she made a typographical error in the letter, I would have

returned it to her to be corrected, which would have robbed her of the full impact of the positive reinforcement. I have found that most people will take the extra moment to check for errors when they know that positive reinforcement will be forthcoming for good work.

Corrective Feedback

Now that you understand how to give positive feedback in a high-impact fashion and the numerous benefits for doing so, the balance you need is how to give corrective feedback in a *positive* manner. The true standards of any organization are not necessarily what are written in the policy manuals. The actual, de facto standard is what we confront in our daily interaction with co-workers and teammates.

If a company advertises to its customers that it is open for business at 8:00 a.m., but no one says anything if an employee arrives by 8:15, even with customers waiting, then everyone learns quickly that 8:15 is the de facto standard. As such, if the employee arrives at 8:20, he or she will hear about it from the boss.

Here is the inevitable bad news. If we do not honor a standard by confronting deviations, then we have, in fact, established a new standard which is less stringent than before. When we decide not to confront a deviation, the standards slip and we lose pride in the organization. This is a truism — high defacto standards create pride in the organization, and lower standards tend to reduce pride. We cannot have it both ways. If this isn't bad enough, there is another compounding problem which this situation creates. We will soon realize that the lower standards, loss of pride, and poor customer service are causing a negative impact on *our* bottom line.

So, in an effort to "pull up our socks" we discipline the next employee who comes to work at 8:10 a.m. by righteously quoting the company policy of 8:00 a.m. Bad decision! Not only is it unfair and unreasonable, but the union could also march us into court with words like "past practice" and "policy through execution." They will win and we will lose.

When we decide to return to the previous standard, then we should assemble everyone concerned, admit we have been lax in the past and then announce, both verbally and in writing, that "starting tomorrow morning, we expect everyone to be at work to serve our customers not later than 8:00 a.m. Anyone arriving later than 8:00 a.m. will be dealt with accordingly." (This means that the boss or leader must be there by 8:00 a.m., also.)

It seems that every organization has someone from Missouri, the "Show Me State." I'll bet you lunch that someone is going to touch the stove to see if it is hot. That person will arrive at 8:15 a.m. If you are going to build pride, leadership credibility, and superior customer service, then the tardy employee should be in your office at 8:16 a.m. taking some appropriate heat.

Giving corrective feedback effectively is an art. A young executive once told me, "Pete, you've really got to teach our staff how to take criticism. Every time I tell them in staff meetings the mistakes they have made, they start an argument." We smile! What this young man did not understand is that there is a direct relationship between how well corrective feedback is taken with the skills of the person giving it. He became my primary focus; he had a great deal to learn about the techniques for giving corrective feedback in a positive manner and in the appropriate setting, i.e., not at staff meetings.

Learn these nine steps and practice them with your team. I will guarantee fewer arguments and a much stronger team spirit.

1.   NEVER, NEVER GIVE CORRECTIVE FEEDBACK IN PUBLIC.

I make very few absolute statements when dealing with people, but that is one. I know of no situation where the long-term disadvantages do not outweigh the short-term benefits for criticizing people in public. They invariably get emotional, defensive, and often childishly irrational.

You should always be in private before attempting the next eight steps or they will not work. The only result you can expect from public criticism is an argument.

2.   CLEARLY AND SPECIFICALLY IDENTIFY AND VALIDATE THE STANDARD THAT HAS BEEN BREACHED.

"Joe, that report is due to me on the twelfth of every month." Do not waffle your comment with something like, "Joe, you need to be paying more attention to deadlines." Simply give it to him in clear language. "Bill, we are required to wear safety goggles whenever we use the grinding wheel."

The next step makes sense only if you do the previous step properly.

3.   DESCRIBE THE DISCREPANCY OR THE INAPPROPRIATE BE-
     HAVIOR.

"Joe, your report is dated the fourteenth" or
"Bill, I noticed you at the grinding wheel without your safety goggles." Now you both know
the specific deviation you need to address. The
discrepancy is usually some performance that is
not up to the minimum standard of quality,
quantity, cost effectiveness, or timeliness.

The fourth step is important when we recall the
truism: "People learn more, learn faster, and make
fewer mistakes when their self-esteem is high."

4.   SEPARATE THE DOER FROM THE DEED.

Say something to indicate that the substandard performance is not normal or expected.
"Joe, I'm very surprised to see that your report
is late. You are usually right on time."

We know that people are more receptive to
corrective feedback when their self-esteem is not
under attack. By separating the person (self-
esteem) from the error or deviation, there is less
chance that he or she will become professionally
embarrassed and defensive.

The next step draws upon the wisdom of
Socrates, one of the world's greatest teachers. He
taught his people by constantly asking them
questions to stimulate their thinking, discovery,
and creativity.

5. ASK AN OPEN, NON-ACCUSATORY QUESTION TO DIS-COVER WHAT ACTUALLY CAUSED THE DEVIATION OR ERROR. "WHAT HAPPENED?"

If we listen carefully, we will probably find that one of the four reasons for non-performance (lack of skill or knowledge, imbalance of consequences, task interference, lack of/poor feedback) caused the deviation. For example, "We are supposed to get an input for our report from the accounting department by the 11th. They had a computer failure and did not send us the data until the 13th; that is why my report was not submitted until the 14th, which was two days late" (task interference).

In most cases, we fix this problem by keeping equipment in good working order. On Joe's part, it is not a question of ability (skills) or willingness (motivation). It is an issue of inadequate resources or inputs.

But what if Joe responds as follows? "Mary usually completes that report, but she is on vacation, and there is no one else in the section who attended the class. So we had no one to complete the report (lack of skill or knowledge). We had to get help from someone in another department who had attended the class. He could not help us until two days after the deadline. That's why we were late."

In order to keep the discussion moving in a constructive direction, ask this question next:

6.   "WHAT DID WE LEARN FROM THIS?"

In order to respond to the question, Joe must rethink the entire situation to look for lessons learned. He might respond by saying, "Well, I have learned that if only one person has the skills to do the report, then I am going to have problems if she is absent when the report is due."

Socrates would advise you to ask this question next.

7.   "WHAT DO YOU RECOMMEND/ SUGGEST THAT WOULD PREVENT HAVING THIS REPORT LATE AGAIN?"

Caution! What may occur next is a risk you can expect to face. I cannot emphasize too strongly how important it is for you to handle the next moment correctly.

Many times the errant employee will feel a bit embarrassed and inadequate at this point. This feeling may provoke a response that plays right into your core of experience and ego. He may say, "I am really not sure what to do; what do you recommend, Boss?"

Let's be honest; you probably got your job because you did Joe's job very well. You, no doubt, have thought of an excellent solution to Joe's problem. But, the broader objective is to solve the problem by letting Joe *own* the solution.

We want Joe, not you, to discover an appropriate solution. Not only will Joe learn more from the experience, but he will be more committed to his own solution than to the one you impose upon him.

When confronted with this temptation to deprive your employee of an excellent learning opportunity, try this response: "Joe, you are a lot more familiar with your situation than I am; I would rather hear your thoughts."

In most instances, this will stimulate Joe's creativity, and he will offer a fine solution, such as: "When Mary returns from vacation, I will ask her to train three of my staff. I will put an asterisk by these names on the sign-out board so I can ensure that one of those trained people is available in the office when the report is due."

What if Joe cannot think of a reasonable solution? In this case, the temptation to offer your solution becomes greater. Unless there is an emergency situation and time is critical, I suggest the following comment: "Well, why not discuss the situation with your staff? Let's get back together after lunch and see what ideas you and your team have come up with."

8. ENSURE THE SOLUTION OFFERED IS SPECIFIC, JOB-RELATED, AND ACTIONABLE.

For example, Joe might say, "Boss, I am sorry we were late; next time we will just try harder." Words like "try harder" are pure fluff! Do not let your people duck a real, actionable solution with fluffy comments like: "We will try harder." Counter with this remark: "I appreciate your willingness to 'try harder,' but what will that look like? Will you be more specific about exactly what you will do to 'try harder'?"

After an appropriate solution has been developed, ask this question:

9.   "WHAT CAN I DO TO HELP?"

Whatever support or resources are re-
quested, make every effort to *over-deliver* on your
commitment. For example, if Joe asks for *one*
copy of the training materials by Thursday so
Mary can conduct the training, I suggest that you
attempt to give him *two* copies on Wednesday,
i.e., over-deliver whenever possible. This dem-
onstrates your high level of interest and support.

10.   CONCLUDE THIS CORRECTIVE FEEDBACK DISCUSSION
WITH A BRIEF RECAP AND SUBSEQUENT FOLLOW-UP.

"Well, Joe, I think you are right. The report
was late because Mary is on vacation—and she
is your only trained employee. I think *your* solution to have her train others will surely prevent
this report from being late in the future. I understand Mary will return on the twelfth. Let's get
together at 2:00 p.m. on the twentieth to see how
the cross-training went."

Put the follow-up appointment on both your
and Joe's calendars. Your specific follow-up time
and date will encourage Joe to have his corrective action completed by that date.

If I feel the need, I put a note on my calendar
a few days prior to our follow-up meeting on the
twentieth to "check" to be sure the corrective
action is underway and on schedule. The phone
call may sound something like this, "Joe, I was
curious how Mary's training is progressing. Do
you need any support from me at this point?"
Assuming all is OK, I conclude with, "Glad to
hear the project is going well; I'm looking for-

ward to our 2:00 p.m. follow-up meeting on the twentieth. Please let me know if I can do anything to help you and Mary."

On rare occasions these corrective actions slip off the person's "worry list" and they suffer from inattention. The above phone call tends to make the scheduled follow-up meeting a much more positive experience for all involved.

As teammates become skillful at giving positive and corrective feedback, they develop a value I call **"CONFRONTATION CREDITS - A KEY TO TEAMWORK."** Let me explain this powerful phenomenon.

You need to think of your relationship with your teammates, also subordinates, as an emotional bank account. All bank accounts are characterized by deposits and withdrawals. You make *emotional* deposits by giving positive feedback, listening, praising, thanking, and the classic "pat-on-the-back." The receivers of such positive behavior will view these as deposits in your emotional bank account with them.

Bear in mind that the value of the deposits is determined by the receiver, not the sender. The terms and expressions the sender uses to convey positive thoughts may not hold the same connotation for the receiver. If possible, learn the specific terms the receiver uses to express positive thoughts. Then use those same terms in response.

Never Overdraw Your Emotional Account

Withdrawals are the things we do which could be perceived negatively by others: giving corrective feedback in public, not listening, interrupting, or taking credit for others' work; the list is lengthy. The key point is that if the receiver considers something as negative, then it is a withdrawal, irrespective of how the sender intended it.

Bottom line—never *overdraw* your emotional account with your teammates! You must be sensitive to the positive contributions of others and express to them your sincere praise and appreciation.

You may recall the rule we had with the Pee Wee Vikings football team, i.e., teammates could only compliment and praise each other. They were not allowed to criticize a fellow teammate. This soon created an overwhelmingly positive confrontation balance and bonded the team together. We heard later that if a kid at school did something bad or made an unkind remark to a Viking player, that person would quickly find that several other Vikings would "encourage" him to stop it.

So, how does this idea of always maintaining a positive confrontation balance relate to teams of adults in business? We have found that in order for individuals to subordinate totally their individual needs and egos for the good of the team, something positive must counterbalance the loss of individual achievement. A strong and sustaining positive confrontation balance among and between teammates tends to serve this purpose.

A Single Heartbeat

Many effective teams understand and effectively use the concept of **"Scotoma,"** which was popularized by Lou Tice at the Pacific Institute in Seattle, Washington. What follows is one of the most important facets of human behavior I have ever learned. It often helps us to understand better why people behave as they do. It explains, in part, why some teams function with a single heartbeat (even in adversity) and why others shatter under pressure.

The human brain has five sensory input channels: smell, taste, touch, hear and see. We function and survive in response to the myriad inputs (stimuli) our five sense organs encounter. While seated in a crowded movie theater, we catch the slightest whiff of smoke. We will perceive that dangerous smell even in the most engrossing movie plot. Good sense dictates that we immediately leave the theater and report what we noticed to the manager. In a word, we *receive* a stimuli (smoke), our brain *perceives* it (we become consciously aware of the potential danger), and we *respond* appropriately (leave the theater and report it).

So far, so good. However, it is not quite that simple. Somewhere in the gray matter of our brains there is something called the Reticular Activating System. This serves as a perceptual filter between our sense organs and that portion of our brains that actually perceives, creating a rational awareness that smoke in a theater represents a threat. This perceptual filter allows only two broad categories of stimuli (sensory inputs) to reach the portion of our brain that creates our perceptions (rational awareness). The two categories are *High Threat* and *High Value*.

In other words, if a stimulus is a threat or is very important to us (high value), the Reticular Activating System will *not* filter it from our perception. However, and more importantly, if the stimuli is considered to be low threat or low value (unimportant), our brain never has an opportunity to perceive it because it is filtered out by our Reticular Activating System. We say we have a scotoma (perceptual filter) for low threat and low value stimuli.

In my seminars, I use the following example to help explain this somewhat abstract concept. Imagine you and a friend are chatting on the sidewalk in the middle of the city. If we were to measure the decibels of your voices and also the decibels of the trucks and cars traveling 15 feet away, which would be louder — your voices or the traffic noise? Yes, the traffic noise would be louder. If that is true, why don't we yell as we chat on the sidewalks? Our helper, scotoma, will filter out much of the traffic noise, so we can chat in conversational tones.

This incredible brain we have will take the two stimuli, your friend's voice and the traffic noise, automatically determine that the voice is of high value, and allow that input to reach the portion of our brain that perceives and understands voice. At the same time, it automatically determines that the traffic noise is low threat/low value and will filter that stimulus from our perception. In a word, we will have a scotoma for the traffic noise.

A Natural Instinct

I think most people can relate to this classic example of how a scotoma serves us well. Imagine a husband and wife in bed asleep at 2:00 a.m. There is a thunderstorm outside, but everyone sleeps despite the loud noises from above. At 2:05 a.m., their two-week old baby in the next room awakens because his breathing has become difficult. You can bet that the mother will bolt out of bed instantly shouting, "Honey, something's wrong with the baby's breathing!" The mother will hear the slightest change in her baby's breathing, even in a thunderstorm. I am confident the psychologists would agree that the ability to perceive when a child is in danger is part of the instinct that comes with motherhood.

In all fairness to husbands, consider this example. The storm rages until 4:00 a.m. when there is a subtle "thump" in the night that is not part of the normal pattern of night sounds. In the following second, the husband will be wide awake and say, "I think I heard someone on the patio." The father has an instinct to protect. I believe the natural instinct to nurture (mom) and protect (dad) started in the Stone Age and will be forever thus.

Our brains are so remarkable that we can, unconsciously, monitor the myriad sensory stimuli we experience continuously; the scotoma (perceptual filter) allows us to get adequate rest during a thunderstorm, while at the same moment, the slightest change in a child's breathing can jolt us from a deep sleep.

The idea of scotoma was driven home to me in 1980 when I was the Vice Commandant of the Air War College, the senior professional school in the United States Air Force at Maxwell AFB in Montgomery, Alabama. It is customary to invite allied nations to send a few senior officers to this nine-month course. There was a Nigerian Brigadier General attending the class in 1980. This general was a fighter pilot, but could easily have played the professional golf tour; he was a gifted athlete.

One Saturday morning, he and three friends were playing on the course near the Alabama River. He had hit his ball into the fairway (where he usually was) and one of his group had sliced his ball into the weeds (where I usually am).

The Nigerian waited patiently on the fairway while the other three players poked around in the rough, trying to find the lost ball. After a few minutes of waiting, the Nigerian walked into the weeds some twenty feet from where his friend was standing. He called out at once, "Joe, look down! There is a snake!" A startled Joe looked between his feet and saw about 6 inches of a snake's tail; that tail was attached to a six-foot water moccasin. Joe was out of the weeds and back on the fairway in one huge leap; he was clearly shaken by that close call with one of the most poisonous snakes in America.

When Joe had regained his composure, he said, "That was amazing. Three of us were standing within a few feet of that water moccasin and never noticed it. You were able to see that tail from 20 feet away. How did you do that?" The Nigerian responded very matter of factly, "Remember, in Nigeria, if you don't see the snake first, you die!" Point. Nigerians do not have a scotoma for a snake, or any part thereof. Anywhere in the world as long as they live — Nigerians always see snakes first.

It is interesting to note that the Nigerian General's visual acuity was probably no better than Joe's. However, Joe did not *perceive* the snake between his feet until the Nigerian pointed it out from 20 feet away.

Sometimes the most subtle signs represent the greatest team building opportunities or threats. The good news is that if you truly value the team, then these subtle signs will be as obvious to you as a snake to a Nigerian.

In summary, we can perceive and thereby react to only those stimuli that are high threat or high value; we never seem to notice (perceive) the countless low threat and low value stimuli in our daily lives. So what does all this have to do with team building? Everything! If teamwork is *very* important to you, you will be able to perceive anything that will help your team or anything that threatens its success.

One of the great benefits of teamwork is that it stimulates creativity. When people are mentally involved in the team activity, they feel personally accountable for the outcome. In a word, the people begin to think creatively because they want to win.

Moscow

One of the saddest moments of my consulting career occurred in 1993 in Moscow while I was on a business trip to several Russian cities. I was in a private meeting with the number two person in Russia's equivalent of our Harvard Business School. As we chatted, through a skilled interpreter, he asked me, "Mr. Land, how do leaders in America get their people to think and be creative? Today in Russia one of our biggest problems is that many of our workers, even our managers, simply fail to think."

"That's a key question," I replied. "The answer I am going to share with you tends to differentiate great organizations from those which are doomed to eventual failure. First, every person in the organization, from the Chairman of the Board to the lowest level hourly employee, must know and personally internalize the mission of the organization. Don't confuse mission with one's job description. The mission is the reason the organization exists."

"Second, there has to be a norm of behavior in which all managers, at all levels, routinely and sincerely ask this question of those reporting directly to them. 'Now that you know our mission, what ideas or suggestions do you have to improve our operation? What do you recommend to help us to accomplish our mission, faster, cheaper, or with higher quality and to improve our service to our customers?' The presidents ask the vice presidents and the foreman asks the hourly craft employees—plus everyone in between.

"You must ask frequently so that they know they will be asked again soon. The natural human response to this subtle pressure is that one begins to think about ways to respond intelligently to the question. Then one day some person will answer with a suggestion that has value in improving the operation. The leader should implement the suggestion and give *public praise* to the individual(s) for the ideas. Then the managers should come to work early the next day because there will be people in their office with ideas for improving the operation."

When I finished that statement, this brilliant Russian educator looked at the floor and said nothing for several moments. Then he spoke, "My friend, there are two reasons why we have problems doing that in Russia. First, in our culture it is not considered 'appropriate behavior' for a manager at one level to ask anyone below himself in the hierarchy a question like that; perhaps that cultural norm can be traced back to when we were ruled by czars whose authority was unquestioned.

"Secondly, and perhaps even more tragic, is the fact that for seventy years, the KGB Secret Police had millions of Russians as underground spies who searched for dissidents. When they learned of someone expressing a view that was not in lock-step with the Communist Party dictates, the person was imprisoned for life in Siberia.

"You see, it was not healthy to make suggestions; you were expected to follow orders and not to question. I see now, Mr. Land, why many Russians have difficulty thinking creatively. First, no one would *ask* for a person's idea. Second, there is no one who would *answer* the question."

This was a profoundly depressing revelation to both of us. But there is a deeper issue—when we know we are not expected to think (and, if we do, it could cost us our freedom) the human mind slips into mental by-pass—we simply do not think!

In my consulting experiences throughout Russia, Europe, the United States, Mexico and Australia, I have found that truly great leaders stimulate their people's minds and bring everyone's potential to bear on their product or service. This process fosters high value for creativity at every level through shared leadership, high-impact feedback, and a positive confrontation balance.

Chapter 5

The Role of Conflict in Team Building

Assume you are holding a card with the word "conflict" written on it. In front of you there are two baskets, one labeled "Positive Concepts," the other labeled "Negative Concepts." If directed to place your card in the appropriate basket, which would you choose? When I pose that question in seminars, the vast majority choose "Negative." In my view, conflict is neither one or it can be either one. How one *handles* conflict determines whether it is viewed as positive or negative. Our goal should be to learn and practice the skills needed to make all conflict situations positive in their impact.

I think it is safe to say that conflict is an integral part of all teamwork; we should not attempt to eliminate it because we cannot. Don't blunt our spear on that fool's errand. As my dad used to say, "The fleas come with the dog." Conflict comes with teamwork. What all good coaches and team leaders have done is develop their skills in managing conflict so as to capitalize on its most positive aspects, while minimizing those negative dimensions which destroy team effectiveness.

The purpose of this chapter is to give you the skills and tools you will need to make conflict, which is inevitable in any team interaction, into a beneficial input for creativity and energy.

"United We Stand"

Over a hundred years ago, our nation divided itself, North against South, and was locked in a bloody civil war. At risk was the survival of our very way of life. President Abraham Lincoln looked at this nation, immersed in negative conflict, and said, "United we stand, divided we fall."

There is a message there for business leaders of today. With this world of intense international competition, often the survival of our organizations is at risk. One of our greatest challenges is to unite all the elements of our organizations and create winning teams.

The information in this chapter will help you, as a leader, create within your workgroup a positive team environment. With you and your people working as a team, all can avoid negative conflict and divisiveness that cause people, who would otherwise be productive, to wallow in mediocrity.

It is necessary to understand that one of the things that has an impact on businesses, that keeps them from doing this, is negative conflict. One of the things we need to understand is that if we are going to win at team building—to better the organization—the first thing we must do is win at managing conflict.

Build Fire in the Workplace

One of the definitions of conflict is "a sharp disagreement of ideas." Thousands of years ago prehistoric man found that by striking flint stones together he could create a spark, and the discovery of fire changed mankind.

There is a useful analogy here. When teams in a positive team environment are having a sharp disagreement of ideas, there is usually a little spark of a new and more creative idea. The very life of creativity comes from conflict.

However, if conflict is allowed to run loose in an organization, for some reason it tends to turn in the negative direction. We become self-serving and self-centered. Our own goals and needs and special agendas become more important than the needs of our organization; teamwork and productivity suffer.

Effective leaders, managers, and coaches can take that same *monster* of negative conflict and turn it around to where it will actually begin to move in a more positive direction. We begin to see a healthy exchange of ideas, sharing a purpose and a oneness of mission which will actually make productivity soar.

In order to help you understand the nature of conflict, please take a moment to study the following model by K. V. Thomas, adapted from his Working

Paper #74-3, "Conflict and Conflict Management" (Figure 5-1).

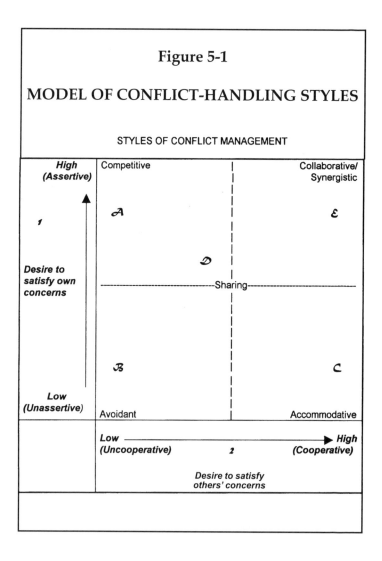

Figure 5-1

MODEL OF CONFLICT-HANDLING STYLES

STYLES OF CONFLICT MANAGEMENT

Figure 5-2

CONFLICT MANAGEMENT STYLE MATRIX

	STYLE	USE IF	AVOID USE IF
A	Competitive	* There is a win-lose reward system * Attainment of one's goals is crucial * Co-acting teams	* Interacting teams * Success requires cooperation * Group reward system
B	Avoidant	* Threat of violence exists * A cooling-off period is appropriate * Confrontation will hurt long-term relationships	* Immediate resolution is needed * One party remains frustrated by the avoidance
C	Accommodative	* Self-sacrifice is valued * Belief in belongingness and group creativity * Harmony is valued	* Excessive dependency may result * Risk taking is needed * Key values are in jeopardy
D	Sharing	* Emphasis on compromise/ negotiation * Differences in goals/values * Balanced power relationships	* May be employed too soon - block creativity
E	Collaborative/ Synergistic	* Desire to integrate interests of all parties * Concern for group goals * High trust, open communications * Creative solutions are valued * Interacting teams	* A solution is needed quickly * Goals are unclear

The model compares the interaction of two variables:

1. The vertical axis is my concern for achieving my goals/needs. If I am very concerned, I will be viewed as behaving in a highly assertive manner. On the other hand, if I have a lower level of concern for my needs, I will be described as being somewhat unassertive.

2. The horizontal dimension has to do with my desire to help others achieve their needs or goals. If I am very interested in helping others, I will be seen as cooperative. In contrast, if I am not the least bit concerned about the other person or group, they will describe me as being uncooperative.

Cooperativeness and Assertiveness

By using Thomas' model, we can understand why people and groups behave as they do. There are five positions on the grid that represent varying degrees of cooperativeness and assertiveness.

Let us assume that I have chosen to be competitive with someone. I move to position (A), competitive, and will be highly assertive and very uncooperative. The style matrix (Figure 5-2) suggests this is appropriate if the other person and I are in a win-lose reward system (opposing teams in a sports contest), where the achievement of one's goals is crucial (second place in the Super Bowl is unacceptable), and we are in a co-acting team environment (trying to win the top sales award).

However, the "avoid use if" column reveals the conditions in which being competitive makes absolutely no sense at all. We should not be competitive within interacting teams (the football players on the same team), where success requires cooperation (a quarterback cannot make a touchdown without the help of the other ten teammates). Finally, avoid competitiveness when there is a group reward system (everyone receives a Super Bowl ring and attends the banquet).

Please study the conflict model plus the style matrix in depth. You will find that there are perfectly appropriate times to be in all positions — (A) competitive, (B) avoidant, (C) accommodative, (D) sharing, and (E) collaborative. And, there are situations in which we should avoid each of these positions.

Now that we understand the model and the associated terms and concepts, I can explain the conflict resolution technique I use to manage conflict within an interacting team situation.

Effective Conflict Resolution

Let us assume that Jack and Jill went up the hill to fetch a pail of water. (It takes both of them working as an interacting team to carry the water safely down the hill). The rest of the team is getting thirsty because Jack and Jill do not get along. In fact, their mutual hostility (conflict) has prevented them from getting the water and has had a negative impact on the entire team's well-being.

This example is useful to explain a simple conflict management technique. You, the team leader, call both Jack and Jill into your office and employ the following steps.

1. Explain the two kinds of teams (co-acting and interacting) and give examples of each.

2. Ask them both: "What type of team is our workgroup—co-acting or interacting?" They will invariably choose interacting.

3. Explain the K. V. Thomas model and the style matrix. Then ask, "Where on this model are the two of you with your present behavior and resulting relationship?"

They always choose some position other than (E) collaborative. This tends to be a moment of truth. They realize that competitive behavior (uncooperative and assertive) is totally dysfunctional with respect to contributing to the interacting team goals.

4. Ask them together, "What new or different behaviors should you **both** do to move your relationship to collaboration/win-win?"

At this point, they will understand the need to change because their present behavior has not and will never produce a win-win relationship for both of them and their teammates.

A note of caution: one party may say, "I'll try harder...." Don't buy that! Agreeing to "try" is fluffy. Respond with, "I appreciate your willingness to 'try harder,' but what will I actually 'see and hear' when you are 'trying harder'? What observable new behavior will we all see?"

5. The next step involves your facilitating a written agreement (contract) that both parties agree to follow which will create a win-win, interacting team relationship. Set specific follow-up dates on all three calendars to ensure that the promises are being kept.

6. As soon as you see the new behaviors, promptly praise the progress with positive feedback.

The following case is a classic example of how unmanaged conflict can lead to devastating consequences. However, when effective conflict resolution is conducted within a team setting, positive results occur.

Teamwork in the Oil Patch

Several years ago, I was contacted by an executive from a major oil company. One of their smaller units in a southern state was experiencing serious conflict. The work climate was so hostile that some people were concerned for their personal safety. There had already been several incidents of fighting and vandalism to personal property and cars. I administered a team evaluation survey and recorded the worst scores I had seen in, at the time, eighteen years of consulting (Appendix C).

During the personal interview phase, I learned the major cause of the hostility. The corporate headquarters in Houston had decreed that each unit manager had to submit a merit ranking of all personnel in descending order. The best employee was ranked number one and the least effective employee would be the last person listed.

The employees on the top portion of the list could expect generous raises, whereas those on the bottom were often terminated. One can well imagine how important each employee's standing on the "hit list" was to his/her future security.

The Tragic Flaw

The tragic flaw in this particular unit was that the senior manager had decided that each person's position on the list was determined by individual knowledge, skills, and contribution. Sounds reasonable, doesn't it? But, let me play out the script to its disastrous conclusion. You may think this is fiction; I wish it were.

The most skilled employee, Jim, knows that his knowledge and individual contribution will help secure his top position on the list and, hence, his future. However, Bob, who had recently joined the company, was assigned to Jim for training. The bad news is that if Jim succeeded in sharing his skills with Bob, then Jim's position on the list was threatened. You can imagine Bob's anger when he learned that Jim was coming back to work at night to keep Bob from learning the "good stuff."

During the confidential personal interview phase of the engagement, I found not only rampant conflict but also open hostility. There were even threats of physical violence.

As I met with the senior executive who was responsible for creating the annual list, he was not surprised that there were many festering conflicts but defended his position as having been directed by corporate headquarters.

I told him that my conducting a team skills workshop was doomed to failure at the outset; no one would even consider using interactive team behavior, which requires cooperation, sharing information, and mutual support. The consequence of such behavior was perceived to be a lower ranking and thus potential termination.

Invert the Order

I suggested a possible solution: "When you introduce me at the start of the workshop, state that you have changed the policy for creating the list. Specifically, the number one person on the list will be the employee who is best at sharing information and skills and helping foster interactive behavior by assisting others. The bottom of the list is reserved for the person who fails to share information and skills. In other words, the best team players get a bonus, and those who grandstand and try to play the 'old game' will probably be fired."

Working and Having Fun

You would be amazed at the enthusiasm for learning the new team skills. The next two days were probably the most exciting I have spent as a trainer. They all wanted lunch catered in so we could work during the lunch break; we stayed in session long after the scheduled closing time.

We had contracted to conduct a follow-up evaluation six months later. We planned to re-administer the survey to compare the before and after results. We tentatively scheduled a refresher/follow-up workshop.

As a result of the exceptionally positive survey, plus performance measures reported by the senior manager, I suggested we cancel the workshop; they were too busy making money for the company. They had recently received recognition from the corporate headquarters in Houston. They were working as an interacting team and having fun doing it.

I have included in Appendix A a more detailed discussion of conflict resolution techniques that you will need if the basic process we have just described fails. However, it has been my experience that this first technique works in the vast majority of cases.

Discipline

Any discussion of conflict would be incomplete if we failed to address the subject of discipline, although in mature high performance teams, discipline is rarely an issue. However, if discipline is needed, what follows is a brief overview of ideas and skills that have served me well over the years.

When most people are asked to label "discipline" as a positive or negative concept, the majority choose negative. I feel it can be negative and often is an unpleasant experience for everyone involved. This is usually because the administration of discipline is done the wrong way for the wrong reasons.

You recall the four broad categories for poor/impaired performance — lack of skill or knowledge, imbalance of consequences, task interference, and lack of/poor feedback. The only situation when discipline is an appropriate solution is when the cause is unwillingness or low motivation (imbalance of consequences).

Team members should never be disciplined if they have not been trained or lack resources (task interference) or are unaware that performance is unacceptable (lack of/poor feedback).

Discipline is primarily a ratcheting down of the negative consequences to effect motivation, (a willingness to start either doing something they should do or stop doing something they should not be doing.)

The Receiver's Value System

A key point to remember is that before consequences can have the desired effect on performance, they must fall within the receiver's value system.

Let's assume an employee is not training employees properly but sincerely enjoys that aspect of his or her job and wants to expand training responsibilities. Any disciplinary action that would reduce or eliminate the training activities would help to motivate the desired change in behavior. Conversely, if you threatened the same consequences to a person who disliked training intensively, you can expect the present unacceptable behavior to continue or get even worse.

When Discipline Is Love

I saw discipline as totally positive after the following experience involving my son, Steve, when he was six years old. I arrived home from my Air Force job one afternoon and noticed Steve was playing in the street. I walked over, took him by the hand and said, "Son, it's not safe for you to play in the street. I love you and do not want you to be hit by a car. You could be hurt badly. So, if I find you playing in the street again, I will have to spank your bottom. Do you understand?" "Yes, Sir," he chirped and off he ran to the backyard.

A week later, I arrived home and found Steve playing in the street. I walked over, took him by the hand and said, "Steve, it appears you are playing in the street again. Do you remember what we talked about last week?"

"Yes Sir," he replied with his eyes staring at his tennis shoes on the asphalt.

I took him in the house, into our bedroom, shut the door and said, "Steve, can you think of any reason why I should not spank your bottom right now?"

"No Sir," he muttered as his eyes filled up with tears in anticipation of the inevitable unpleasant consequences for playing in the street again.

I turned him across my knees and proceeded to administer a few firm swats of discipline. He cried but it always hurt me more. In a few minutes, he was in the backyard playing happily; I was still hurting.

Over a month later, on a Saturday morning, I was down on one knee trimming the grass along the driveway, and Steve was playing in the front yard. There was an Air Force major who lived across the street. He was in his front yard and his young son was playing in the street. If I live to be one hundred years old, I will never forget what happened next. Steve walked over, put his hand on my shoulder and said, "Dad, isn't it sad that Major Evans doesn't love his son as much as you love me."

Bingo! Discipline, when done properly and for the right reasons, is not only positive but can be considered an act of love.

Dick Leatherman's Modules

Allow me to share with you a few techniques to make discipline a truly positive experience for all concerned, especially the team.

One of my most respected mentors is Dr. Dick Leatherman, Chairman of International Training Consultants in Richmond, Virginia. His training material on "Taking Disciplinary Action" is the best I have seen in my twenty years of consulting. Dick Leatherman's modules are unique because they represent the best practices of executives and managers who excel at such critical skills as administering discipline. While Dick's material is well grounded in the managerial concepts and principles, he devotes the lion's share of his offerings to teaching you, the student, the discreet skills you need to practice to do the task correctly. I have taught thousands of managers and supervisors *how* to discipline someone using Dick Leatherman's material. Does it really work? The following story is representative of scores I have received.

A few years ago I conducted a "How To Administer Discipline In A Positive Manner" workshop. A new manager in his mid-twenties was in attendance. Several weeks later it became necessary for him to discipline an hourly employee who was 24-years his senior. He called to relate this story:

I was nervous about having to discipline Bill because he is much older than I, and he helped train me when I joined the company. I re-read my notes and the booklet from your work-shop.

I completed my preparation forms then discussed my decision with my boss and our company attorney. They felt I was handling the situation in a manner that was fair to our team and to Bill, also.

I met with Bill and used the eight-step Leatherman model you taught us. The session went quite well. Much to my surprise, as we rose to leave, Bill said, "John, I am disappointed with my performance, and I am sorry I have let the team down. But, you certainly handled this situation with a lot of class."

He shook my hand warmly and promised to take the appropriate corrective action. His performance has been exemplary. We are even closer than we were before the discipline situation.

Does this sound like a fairy tale? It isn't. I have received many similar calls. If you want the full course, call International Training Consultants and purchase the module; it will be one of the best investments you will ever make.

With Dick's permission, I will share the highlights of the process:

1. Describe the Discrepancy
   a. Describe the problem.
   b. Refrain from blaming the employee.

2. Review previous discussions and agreement.

    a. Before the meeting, review your notes regarding the required improvement, identified causes of the problem, agreed-to solutions and actual results.

    b. During the meeting review the standard expected, causes of the problem identified in prior meetings, solutions agreed to in prior meetings and current lack of results.

3. Ask employee why performance has not improved.

4. Listen and respond to employee's feelings. Let the employee know you understand how he or she feels even though you may not agree with the reasons for these feelings.

5 Indicate the disciplinary action you are taking.

    a. Penalty should meet the requirements of the organization's policy for progressive discipline.

    b. Let the employee know that the purpose of the discipline is to get him or her to make the improvement discussed in prior meetings, not punishment for past failures.

6. Agree on a solution to the problem.

    a. Encourage the employee to develop his or her own solution with suggestions from you.

    b. If appropriate, set up a timetable for improvement.

7. Specifically indicate additional discipline to be taken if there is no improvement.

8. Indicate confidence that employee will improve.

Chapter 6

A Team Building Process That Really Works

I have read dozens of books on team building; each scholar presents overwhelming evidence to support his or her particular process. However, the next book I read offers an equally convincing position on how to build teams, which is quite different from the previous book, and so it goes. What this litany of divergent opinions has taught me is that nobody has found the one best way yet, and maybe no one ever will.

I do not presume that my way is best. Instead, I have sifted through the literature to glean those techniques which appear to be solidly grounded in common sense and reality, as opposed to more interesting and stimulating theories. I then add the biases I have developed through my sixty-four years of dealing with people. My biases include such notions as: "Most people want to do a good job; Most people need recognition for honest good work; Most people want to be respected by people they themselves respect; And, most people want to win."

Steps to Follow

What follows is a blow-by-blow description of how I, as an external management consultant, conduct a team building engagement in a client organization. Of course, some of these steps would not be necessary or appropriate if you are a member of the organization or an internal consultant and are familiar with the organization's culture, history, values, and key leaders.

Since my perspective and experience is that of an external consultant/facilitator, anyone in a similar position should conduct the Phase I — Background Orientation. In-house team leaders, coaches, or consultants will need to modify this procedure somewhat but should make every effort to follow the overall intent of this strategy — because it works!

Like people in any profession, I stand on the shoulders of my professional forebears; people publish their ideas for others to use. There is a relatively new team skills assessment instrument developed by Paul O'Keefe and his talented team at Edge Training Systems, Inc., in Richmond, VA. His "Knowledge for Teams" uses eighty-nine multiple-choice questions to assess the team member's knowledge in six key dimensions: communication, coordination, collaboration, cooperation, change, and coaching.

The computer scoring system reveals an accurate diagnosis of the team's strengths and needs. A more complete description of this fine assessment tool is contained in Appendix E.

Two authors who have provided me with a superb team building assessment instrument are Dave Francis and Don Young; their book, *Improving Workgroups* is a practical, no-nonsense book on the subject. I will discuss exactly how I use their "Team Effectiveness Questionnaire" (Appendix C) a bit later, but first let us introduce a workable team-building process.

The Recipe

What I am going to share with you is the team-building process that I have used successfully for many years with a wide variety of organizations — from governmental agencies to Fortune 500 companies — from Little League Sports to combat units in the Vietnam conflict. I can say without fear of contradiction that this system really works. However, remember the cake analogy — if you do not follow this procedure (recipe) carefully, you could have less than satisfactory results.

You can never sell team building to an organization unless there is a perceived need for better teamwork within the organization. In every case, someone has contacted me and asked for help in building a team.

One pre-condition is the unsettling feeling within the organization that the present, and often traditional, values are no longer serving them well. They sense conflict and competitiveness within the group, which divert energy and attention away from taking care of the customer or the mission.

Coaches Are Teachers

Several years ago, a vice president of a large manufacturing company called me. At our first meeting, he explained, "I have been reading about how teamwork improves productivity, so I want you to build a team in my division."

I explained that his role as vice president would have to shift away from supervising and directing the operation toward a coaching position. He inquired, "What's the difference between supervising and coaching?"

I responded, "Coaches are teachers. In most healthy organizations, people are often promoted to the next higher position because they excelled at the job they previously held. In essence, you, as vice president, represent excellence in your previous position of department head. When you assume the role of coach, you help the people in the job you held (department head) become *better* at that job than you were when you were a department head.

"Coaches willingly share their lessons learned so the new Department Head can benefit from the coach's successes and failures and reach even higher levels of excellence.

"Remember, the coach does not want his/her people only to be good; they must become *better*. Coaches develop their teammates' abilities, so they can delegate considerable decision-making authority to them.

"Coaches create a 'good-finding' environment,

rather than a 'fault-finding' atmosphere. As a coach, you would 'ask' instead of 'tell,' and would create a climate of self-discovery through your skills in asking questions."

The longer I talked, the more agitated he became. He interrupted, "Wait a minute! I have had every job in this division and excelled at all of them. I know more about this operation than anyone here. I am not about to give my authority to people less qualified than I am. I am not interested in coaching; I run this division and will continue to do so. But I still want you to build a team."

Coaches Support the Team

I looked him straight in the eye and said, "The leader's behavior that creates and supports teams is *coaching*, not the traditional *supervision* you describe. Remember—supervision begets employees who often go home on time; coaching begets teammates who focus on the mission not the clock—and that is the way it is.

"We never described Coach Bear Bryant as the president or supervisor of the Alabama football team. Today you must choose whether you want to be a supervisor and have employees working *for* you or whether you want to become a coach and have teammates working *with* you. Pick one."

"Damn it, Pete, I am not going to give away the authority I have worked my whole career to earn."

"Well," I replied, "I have enjoyed the chat and the coffee, but I cannot help you." I left. I was not surprised to learn a few months later that he had been out-placed.

When I am called to assist an organization with building an effective team, I generally follow a series of phased activities.

Phase I — Background Orientation

Before going on site, I ask the contact person in the client organization (hopefully, the CEO or President) to send me the following information:

1. Résumés of the prospective teammates

2. Two of the most recent quarterly reports

3. Current annual report

4. Organizational chart of at least the top three levels with names of incumbents

5. Last three newsletters or equivalent

6. Representative sales and marketing brochures

7. Any other information they feel would help me understand their organization's unique culture

I study this information and research any trade journal articles of interest about the industry and/or the client organization. The Internet is a good research source, as well. Of course, internal consultants could abbreviate this phase.

Phase II — Initial Briefing and Survey

I meet with the group and explain, in detail, the team building goals (see Appendix B). What follows is a frank dialogue about the benefits, risks, and need to effect lasting change in the organization.

I share with them the old adage: "If you always do what you have always done, then you will always get what you have always gotten." I stress that present and past activities, behaviors, values, and relationships have produced a condition which does not seem to serve them well. I then stress in polite, but unequivocal, terms that unless everyone is committed to the change process, from the outset, that I will terminate the engagement at that moment, because if we proceed without everyone "in the boat," all the next few months will produce is wasted time and money, additional stress, and destructive conflict.

Invariably, the group will soon revert to the old patterns of behavior; in a word, it will result in a totally negative experience for all involved, including me. This probably sounds confrontational and a tad blunt. What I am really doing is similar in the sales process to "asking for the order." The client needs to know that you, as the consultant, are willing to walk away from the potential fees before you will participate in a losing situation.

On occasion, I have excused myself from the meeting so as a group they can caucus on the question. I am happy to report that, so far, my client groups have unanimously agreed. This agreement can also be referred to in later sessions when I detect signs of backsliding and resistance to change.

I close that meeting by distributing to each member the Young and Francis "Team Review Questionnaire" and answer sheet (see Appendix C) plus a stamped envelope addressed to my office. The group is asked to complete the questionnaire without any contact or discussion with others and mail their answer sheets to me within one week.

Phase III — Analysis

I conduct an analysis of their responses per the instructions in the appendix. The best possible score on any dimension is 0, which means that every respondent felt that dimension to be a positive aspect of the group. Conversely, the worst possible result is 9.0 which indicates that 100% of the respondents felt that dimension to be a significant problem area.

I normally select the top three strengths to use for building the team. For example, if the group feels inter-group relations to be strong, then any later activities should certainly not have a negative impact on inter-group relations but should further strengthen them. We often find that groups becoming teams need a shared strength they can fall back on when the going gets tough.

I also identify the three weakest dimensions, i.e., the dimensions with the highest scores. These will be probed during the next phase.

Phase IV — Confidential Interviews

Confidential sensing interviews, approximately one hour in duration, are scheduled with each member of the group. In these one-on-one sessions, my purpose is to offer general feedback on the Questionnaire results and probe to find out *why* the strengths and weaknesses exist.

When someone appears reluctant to level with me, I restate the fact that the systemic issues I surface will be worked with the group, but no one's name is ever mentioned.

If still guarded in candor, I say something like this, "I sense you are uncomfortable sharing certain matters with me. I admire your professionalism for not wanting to 'air your dirty laundry in public.'

"However, my relationship with this group is analogous to your relationship with your physician. When he asks, 'Where does it hurt?' you quickly assist him in the diagnosis so he can prescribe a prompt and effective cure.

"Think of me as an organizational doctor and the group as my patient. My ability to help this group become an effective and productive team is determined, in large measure, by how honestly all the group members tell me 'where it hurts'!

"One can only imagine your state of health if your physician were told only partial or inaccurate symptoms."

This frame of reference always makes the interviewee feel not only professionally confident but also quite willing to unload the unvarnished facts and perceptions. This outpouring of facts and feelings is often cathartic and helps build trust between the consultant and the client.

These interviews include such questions as follows:

1. "If you were king/queen for a day, and you could make any *one* change in the team's operation to make it more effective, what specifically would you do and exactly how would you implement such a change?"

2. "What one thing could *you* personally do to help your team?"

3. "On a scale of 1-10 (10 = high), where do you perceive the group to be in 'team spirit'? What could be done to enhance team spirit?"

Phase V — Team Assessment

After concluding all sensing interviews, I conduct a final team assessment integrating the interview notes, questionnaire data, my personal observations, and all the previously provided information.

This is the most demanding facet for me, both personally and professionally. I must suppress the prejudices and subjective feelings I have developed thus far in the engagement; I will like some of the teammates more than others; some of them will like me more than others. It is time to park the ego at the door because you must call the situation as objectively as you can.

I will write my team assessment report and then allow it to "cool" a few days. Then I review and fine-tune it, as necessary. I have found that a little time and distance from the project improves the product.

As with physicians, the power is in the diagnosis. If they misdiagnose the malady, there is no way to cure the sickness. It is the same with team building. Devoting great attention to nailing the assessment will save a lot of misdirected energy chasing the wrong rabbit.

One final word about the importance of a thorough, complete, and accurate assessment. When you return to conduct the outbriefing with the team, your professional credibility is on the line.

If they suspect your assessment to be in error, nothing else good happens. However, if the outbrief is a positive "ah-ha" experience, they will not only have confidence in you to guide the subsequent team building activities, but they will also feel a sense of ownership and mutual respect for each other by knowing that you could not have nailed the assessment without everyone's candor and forthrightness in the questionnaire and interviews. Yes, this is the beginning of building a team culture; they work together to assist in their own diagnosis.

Phase VI — Feedback and Action Planning

I normally meet briefly with the senior executive to pre-brief him or her on the assessment results. This is particularly important if I need to provide some constructive feedback to that person. They value the candor but truly appreciate this one-on-one relationship to discuss personal opportunities for growth. Often the senior executive gets the least objective feedback of the entire management team. Since we are all flawed, yes, even CEOs, we can all benefit from shining light in dark corners.

One subtle strategy with my pre-briefing is to

develop a partnership with this person so that my briefing to the group is actually a team effort. The CEO can assist me in explaining the issues raised. In a word, we put the CEO's spin on the briefing.

Next, we meet with the assembled team. With the use of professionally prepared overhead transparencies, I conduct a formal briefing on:

1. The overall process, all seven phases.

2. The aggregated questionnaire results.

3. An overview of the interview results.

4. My assessment of the team's present strengths and opportunities for growth.

5. I present the proposed workshop agenda and explain exactly how each of the team building goals will be achieved.

6. With help from the CEO, we schedule a workshop date, which is acceptable to all members. If anyone cannot attend on a suggested date, a new date is proposed. I cannot overemphasize the importance of everyone on the team being in attendance.

Each team building session is unique since every team has its own special strengths and needs. If goal setting is a need, we develop specific goals; if communication is a problem, we work on that issue and so it goes.

I have included in Appendix D a process I have used many times to help resolve conflict between departments. The technique requires a skilled facilitator but the results have been impressive.

Phase VII — Workshop, Training, Follow-up

The next phase is the actual team building workshop. Do not attempt this within the company facilities; go off-site for one or two days. The best results I have experienced were at a resort or training facility away from phones, secretaries, and the trappings of power. It is all right to have an evening meal together, but limit the amount, if any, of alcohol that is served.

At the conclusion of the workshop, have the CEO announce that the consultant will return to reassess the team in four to six months. At the time, he or she expects the new team behavior to have become the norm — a new way of doing business.

I always teach positive and corrective feedback skills in the workshop so that any new, positive team behaviors can be reinforced immediately. Teammates also need the skills to confront unacceptable behavior quickly and professionally. This "instant reinforcement" tends to help everyone through the "fuzzy phase" of adjusting to new behaviors and skills.

This seven-phase team building strategy is the result of many years of study, experience, success, and failure. There is nothing new or novel here except the possible blending of the best ideas from many people who are brighter than I am.

My contribution to you is the many lessons I have learned the hard way. I share them with you here with my best wishes. I am sure you and I desire the same thing — a vibrant and energetic team accomplishing great things. This process has helped me

and my clients achieve such objectives. I am confident it will serve you equally well.

Epilogue

Concluding Thoughts

As we look over our shoulder, we now understand the basic team concepts, values, elements, and characteristics; we see how they may clash with our American culture of rugged individualism. We understand a process or recipe to blend the most successful team building practices with generous portions of common sense. We have evidence that the process can help create high performance teams from state governments, to multinational corporations, to the Olympics, to combat units in wartime.

I want to share a few concluding thoughts. Successful businesses are *not* built on satisfied customers. They are built on *enthusiastic* customers. Yes, you have heard all your business life that if you meet (or satisfy) your customers' needs, they will return and remain loyal—hence, success for your business. That was true several years ago, but intense competition, as well as sophisticated and demanding customers, have created an environment that soon purges the marketplace of companies who fail to satisfy basic customer needs. In a word, customer satisfaction is the right-of-passage to simple survival. So, if a company is still in business, that means the company is meeting customers' needs or satisfying them.

Today the game of business success is played on a completely different field than in the past. The minimum level of performance is to satisfy basic customer expectations. In actuality, there are three kinds of customers, and we have all played those roles on occasion.

First, a dissatisfied customer does not get needs met. For example, you are seated in a restaurant and you open the menu and see an entree priced at $10. You think if you order that item, you will receive a meal worth roughly $10 *in your value system.*

The concept of value systems is important because people often ascribe different values based on their specific need level at that moment.

How much would you pay for a glass of water if you were in a desert and had not had any water for two days?

Imagine what you would pay for that same glass of water standing neck deep in a swimming pool in a rainstorm having just finished a six-pack of chilled beer. The example is a bit extreme, but it makes the point that worth and value lie in the fickle mind of the customer.

Now, back to the restaurant. In the next hour the hot food was cold; the cold food was hot; the silverware was dirty; the table was sticky; the waiter rarely came to the table and was surly when he did. You have just had a $3 experience in your value system, but the bill read $10. You learned fairness and equity at your mother's knee and you figure if you pay $10, you have been ripped off to the tune of $7.

How do you respond? Pay $3 and leave? No. Provide some pointed feedback to the waiter and manager and demand $7 be deducted from your bill? Probably not, since our parents also taught us not to make a scene.What most dissatisfied customers do when they get ripped off is the following:

1. As the restaurant disappears in the rear-view mirror, they make a life-long pledge: "You will never get me again!!"

2. Research reveals that dissatisfied customers push negative information about that restaurant to as many as twelve associates, colleagues, and friends. Every time we tell someone about that lousy restaurant, we level the imbalance in our value system against that restaurant. After we've told nine to twelve people the horror story, we now feel better. The account is even; we can forget about the dissatisfying experience.

The second kind of customer is a *satisfied customer*. You have a $10 expectation, and they deliver a $10 experience in your value system. When we get what we pay for, we soon forget the experience. We will return if it is convenient but will not go out of our way; we are moderately loyal and will offer a positive recommendation if specifically asked. This is how satisfied customers generally behave. And, remember, all businesses are creating satisfied customers.

The final and finest kind of customer is an *enthusiastic customer*. I can best explain how enthusiastic customers are created and how they contribute to the inevitable success of a business by relating a personal experience.

Several summers ago, I was invited to address a group at the Federal Executive Institute in Oak Ridge, Tennessee. I planned to fly our company aircraft into the Knoxville Airport the afternoon before my speech the next morning. My contact person invited me to join the group for dinner at Grady's Restaurant in Knoxville at 5:30 p.m.

I asked, "Why so early?" She indicated that they wanted the group to experience the "Legendary Service" for which that restaurant was known. She explained that Grady's was providing an early private seating at 5:30, because a group that large could not be seated at 7:30 without a two-hour wait, due to large crowds every evening. As an experienced traveler, I was skeptical about experiencing "Legendary Service." I have heard a lot of talk but rarely seen the walk.

I landed at the airport and took a taxi to Grady's, arriving around 5:45 p.m. The hostess asked for my name and seated me at a table with members of our group. In the process, she told the young waiter, Joe, my name. He approached, "Mr. Land, what may I bring you to drink?"

"I'd like a large glass of unsweetened iced tea with lemon, please." He was back in a flash and took my order in a very professional and courteous manner. After this hot traveler had gulped the glass of tea, I looked up to see a smiling Joe standing at our table. "Mr. Land, would you like another glass of unsweetened iced tea with lemon?"

"Yes, I certainly would."

He removed the empty glass with his left hand and simultaneously replaced it with a full glass which he had hidden in his right hand behind his back. In the next hour, I was treated to an outstanding dining experience — the hot food was hot, and the cold food was cold; the table was squeaky clean — you get the picture.

The entire staff at Grady's Restaurant walked the talk of "Legendary Service." The bill was $20, but I had received a $30 experience in my value system. I received far more than I paid for.

The good news is that our innate sense of fairness creates an imbalance in our minds in favor of the restaurant. We feel we owe them something in addition to the $20 plus a generous tip. How do we even the account?

1.   As the restaurant disappears in the rear view mirror, we make a pledge: "I can't wait to come back and bring a friend."

2.   We tell others about the great experience. However, research reveals that only one third of the people who hear the horror stories will be told the great experience. It is true: only three to four people will benefit from enthusiastic customers.

To bring into focus many of the ideas we have shared in this book, let us examine more closely a normal daily experience to learn how wonderfully our minds perceive our environment to create either dissatisfied, satisfied, or enthusiastic customers.

Imagine you are on your daily commute, complete with freeway traffic, billboards, and your favorite radio program. Suddenly you see a new billboard which touts the "great food and excellent service" of the restaurant that "ripped you off" several months ago. Your reticular activating system will *not* filter that sign from your perception (scotoma) because of your personal unpleasant experience. The sign will remind you to tell several more people about that lousy restaurant — dissatisfied customers help create bankruptcies.

But, the converse is also true; if that restaurant had made you an enthusiastic customer, you will perceive the billboard (no scotoma), which will remind you to tell others about that *great* restaurant.

Successful businesses are built on the inevitable and inescapable actions of enthusiastic customers — enthusiastic customers are created by the integrated actions of teams. I think a good way to bring this book to a close is to show how the Grady's leaders did what is absolutely necessary to build a high performance team that routinely delivers legendary service.

Every person on the team had internalized their charter — "create enthusiastic customers!" The chef was trained, motivated and equipped to do that. He was provided the freshest and highest quality ingredients and would accept nothing less because substandard ingredients do not create enthusiastic customers. The waiter noticed the perspiration on my brow and the enthusiasm with which I asked for a glass of iced tea. He knew a second glass would help make me enthusiastic. The busboy, perhaps the lowest paid teammate, would not even consider leaving the table just a little sticky; he gets a fresh sponge and clean water to leave the table squeaky clean.

The profound difference between good teams and truly great teams lies in the "intangibles," those shared feelings of mutual respect, trust, and complete confidence in one another.

The Grady's team reflects these all-important intangibles. The waiter would have bet his last paycheck that the food prepared by the chef would be absolutely delicious (made with only the freshest ingredients). The chef was sure that the waiters would serve the hot meal quickly and professionally. The waiters knew full well that the busboys would have a spotless table properly set for every guest. Each member of the team (chef, waiter, and busboy) is proud of each teammate for his or her unique and important contribution to dining excellence.

The traditional hierarchies of status and position power fade in the mindset of truly great teams. Of course, we need a focus of leadership—someone to call the plays in the huddle, but there is an overriding common spirit that binds the team with intangible bonds which are far stronger than rules, positions, job descriptions, titles, and position power. When individuals perform in an outstanding manner, they may justifiably say to themselves, silently, "Damn, I'm good!" However, when mature teams produce incredible collective results, every teammate can justifiably shout aloud, "Damn, we're good!"

Each one of Grady's teammates sees the interact-

ing nature of the organization; therefore, each is committed and accountable for achieving the team's charter — "to create enthusiastic customers who tell others about our Legendary Service."
...And, oh yes, they have fun doing it!

Appendix A

Conflict Resolution Techniques

$\big($see Chapter 5$\big)$

Here is a conflict resolution technique for improving understanding and communication between the parties. The process is called "mutual paraphrasing" and requires a skilled facilitator. Here's how it works:

1. The facilitator and the two parties (Mary and Joe) sit in a triangular arrangement in which there is no table or furniture separating the three people.

2. The facilitator explains the process in complete detail to ensure both parties understand the ground rules. I suggest something like this:

"Joe, Mary, it has become obvious to me that one root cause of the conflict the two of you are experiencing is the fact that there is a breakdown in communication. In order to improve the situation, we are going to conduct an activity called mutual paraphrasing. Each of you will have equal opportunity, but I want to start with Mary.

For the next few minutes, Mary, I want you to look at me and, as succinctly and unemotionally as possible, describe to me the major issues and concerns you have with Joe and his organization.

Joe, while Mary is explaining her concerns, your task is to listen carefully, take notes; do not interrupt.

After she completes her statement, you must paraphrase to *me* what Mary told me until she *agrees* with you that your summary is essentially what she said. Resist the temptation to make editorial comments. You are simply to restate the essence of her position until she is satisfied with your review of her statement.

Next, Joe, you will have an equal opportunity to explain to me as succinctly and unemotionally as possible, your concerns with Mary and her organization.

Mary, you must listen, take notes, and not interrupt. After Joe has explained his position to me, you must paraphrase his position until he agrees and accepts your restatement of his concerns. Remember, both of you are directing your remarks to me, not to each other."

I have used this technique many times when the situation has deteriorated to the point that the emotional tension has all but destroyed each party's ability to communicate effectively. The facilitator must draw on his/her position power to maintain a disciplined environment.

This technique literally forces the parties to listen for understanding and reduces the emotional barriers. Often, this is the first time in months both parties actually understand the problem from the other's perspective. In my consulting, this technique has often been a turning point in the resolution of the conflict. A reasonable solution quickly follows.

Appendix B

Team Building Goals

(see Chapter 6)

Certain task and interpersonal issues impede a team's functioning. Team building aims at improving the problem-solving ability among team members by working through these issues. This major goal includes a number of subgoals:

1. A better understanding of each team member's role in the work group.

2. A better understanding of the team's charter — its purpose and role in the total functioning of the organization.

3. Increased communication among team members about issues that affect the efficiency of the group.

4. Greater support among group members.

5. A clearer understanding of group process — the behavior and dynamics of any group that works closely together.

6. More effective ways of working through problems inherent to the team — at both task and interpersonal levels.

7. The ability to use conflict in a positive rather than a destructive way.

8. Greater collaboration among team members and the reduction of competition that is costly to the individual, group, and organization.

9. A group's increased ability to work with other work groups in the organization.

10. A sense of interdependence among group members.

The final aim of team building, then, is a more cohesive, mutually supportive, and trusting group that will have high expectations for task accomplishment and will, at the same time, respect individual differences in values, personalities, skills, and idiosyncratic behavior. Successful team building should nurture individual potential.

(This is a copy of a handout given to me over fifteen years ago by a seminar attendee. It is not my material; it had no author's name. Many thanks to the person who compiled this list of team building goals.)

Appendix C

The Team-Review Questionnaire

(see Chapter 6)

Instructions

You will find 108 statements listed. Think about each statement in relation to the Director's Senior Staff. Use the Team-Review Questionnaire Answer Sheet to respond to the statements. If you feel that a statement is broadly true, mark an X on the appropriate number in the answer sheet grid. If you feel that a statement is not broadly true, then leave that number blank.

Work methodically through the questionnaire, answering each question. There may be times when you find it difficult to answer a particular question but come to the best answer you can. It might be useful to note in the margin the numbers of these difficult questions.

Remember that the quality of the result is directly related to your own openness when answering the questions. This is not meant to be a scientific survey, but rather it serves as a tool to provoke thought and discussion.

TEAM-REVIEW QUESTIONNAIRE

1. The team's manager and members spend little time in clarifying what they expect and need from one another.

2. The work of the team would improve if members upgraded their technical qualifications.

3. Most of the members feel that the aims of the team are hardly worthwhile.

4. People in this team often are not really frank and open with each other.

5. The objectives of our team are not really clear.

6. Team members are unsure about the team's contribution to the wider organization.

7. We rarely achieve much progress in team meetings.

8. The objectives of some individual team members do not gel with those of other members.

9. When team members are criticized, they often feel that they have lost face.

10. New members often are just left to find their own place in the team.

11. Not many new ideas are generated by the team.

12. Conflicts between our team and other groups are quite common.

13. The team manager rarely tolerates leadership efforts by other team members.

14. Some team members are unable to handle the current requirements of their work.

15. Team members are not really committed to the success of the team.

16. In group discussion, team members often hide their real motives.

17. In practice, the team rarely achieves its objectives.

18. Our team's contribution is not clearly understood by other parts of the organization.

19. When the team is having a meeting, we do not listen to each other.

20. Team members are uncertain about their individual roles in relation to the team.

21. Members often restrain their critical remarks to avoid "rocking the boat."

22. The potential of some team members is not being developed.

23. Team members are wary about suggesting new ideas.

24. Our team does not have constructive relationships with some of the other teams within the organization.

25. Team members are uncertain where they stand with the team manager.

26. Our mix of skills is inappropriate to the work we are doing.

27. I do not feel a strong sense of belonging to the team.

28. It would be helpful if the team could have "clear-the-air" sessions more often.

29. In practice, low levels of achievement are accepted.

30. If the team were disbanded, the organization would not feel the loss.

31. The team meetings often seem to lack a methodical approach.

32. There is no regular review of individual objectives and priorities.

33. The team is not good at learning from its mistakes.

34. Team members tend not to show initiative in keeping up-to-date or in developing themselves.

35. We have the reputation of being stick-in-the-muds.

36. The team does not respond sufficiently to the needs of other teams in the organization.

37. The team manager gets little information about how the team sees his performance.

38. People outside the team consider us unqualified to meet work requirements.

39. I am not prepared to put myself out for the team.

40. Important issues often are "swept under the carpet" and not worked through.

41. Individuals are given few incentives to stretch themselves.

42. There is confusion between the work of this team and the work of others.

43. Team members rarely plan or prepare for meetings.

44. If team members are missing, their work just does not get done.

45. Attempts to review events critically are seen as negative and harmful.

46. Little time and effort is spent on individual development and training.

47. This team seldom innovates anything.

48. We do not actively seek to develop our working relationships with other teams.

49. The team would get better quality decisions if the team members took the initiative.

50. The team's total level of ability is too low.

51. Some team members find it difficult to commit themselves to doing the job well.

52. There is too much stress placed on conformity.

53. Energy is absorbed in unproductive ways and does not go into getting results.

54. The role of our team is not clearly identified within the organization.

55. The team does not set aside time to consider and review how it tackles problems.

56. Much improvement is needed in communication between team members.

57. We would benefit from an impartial assessment of how we work.

58.   Most team members have been trained only in their technical discipline.

59.   Good ideas seem to get lost.

60.   Some significant mistakes would have been avoided if we had better communication with other teams.

61.   The team manager often makes decisions without talking them through with the team.

62.   We need an input of new knowledge and skills to make the team complete.

63.   I wish I could feel more motivated by working in this team.

64.   Differences between team members rarely are properly worked through.

65.   No time is devoted to questioning whether our efforts have been worthwhile.

66.   We do not have an adequate way to establish our team's objectives and strategy.

67.   We often seem to get bogged down when a difficult problem is being discussed in team meetings.

68.   The team does not have adequate administrative resources and procedures.

69.   We lack the skills to review our effectiveness constructively.

70. The team does not take steps to develop its members.

71. New ideas from outside the team seldom are accepted.

72. In this organization, teams and departments tend to compete rather than collaborate.

73. The team manager does not adapt his style to changing circumstances.

74. New people coming into the team sometimes lack the necessary qualifications.

75. No one is trying hard to make this a winning team.

76. Individuals in this team do not really get to know each other as people.

77. We seem more concerned about giving a good appearance than achieving results.

78. The organization does not use the vision and skills that the team has to offer.

79. We have team meetings, but do not properly examine their purpose.

80. We function in rather a rigid manner and are not sufficiently flexible in using team resources.

81. Performance would improve if constructive criticism were encouraged.

82. Individuals who are retiring or uncertain often are overridden.

83. It would be fair to say that the team has little vision.

84. Some of the other teams/departments seem to have a low opinion of us.

85. The team manager is not sufficiently sensitive to the different needs of each member.

86. Some team members are not adapting to the needs of the team, despite efforts to help them.

87. If a team member gets into difficulties, he usually is left to cope with them by himself.

88. There are cliques and political maneuvering in the team.

89. Nothing that we do could be described as excellent.

90. The team's objectives have not been systematically related to the objectives of the whole organization.

91. Decisions made at meetings are not properly recorded or activated.

92. Team members could collaborate much more if they examined the possibilities of doing so on a person-by-person basis.

93. Little time is spent on reviewing what the team does, how it works, and how to improve it.

94. A person who questions the established practices in the team probably will be smartly put back in place.

95. Only a few members suggest new ideas.

96. We do not get to know the people working in other teams in the organization.

97. I do not know whether our team is adequately represented at higher levels.

98. Some team members need considerable development to do their work effectively.

99. Team members are committed to individual goals at the expense of the team.

100. Disagreements between team members are seldom worked through thoroughly and individual view-points are not fully heard.

101. We often fail to finish things satisfactorily.

102. We do not work within clear strategic guidelines.

103. Our meetings do not properly resolve all the issues that should be dealt with.

104. We do not examine how the team spends its time and energy.

105. We make resolutions but, basically, we don't learn from our mistakes.

106. Individuals are not encouraged to go outside the team to widen their personal knowledge and skill.

107. Creative ideas often are not followed through to definite action.

108. If we worked better with other teams, it would help us all to be more effective.

TEAM-REVIEW QUESTIONNAIRE INTERPRETATION

Each answer sheet should be scored as follows. Add the number of X's in each vertical column and write the total in the box above the Roman numerals. You will have a total figure for each of the twelve columns. After totaling all answer sheets, then find the group average for each of the twelve dimensions.

The worst possible average score is 9, which means every person placed an X in every box in that particular column.

Conversely, the best possible score is 0, which means that none of the respondents felt any of the statements in a particular column fairly represented his/her team. Since the survey is composed of negative statements, failure to agree is, in fact, a positive response.

When you conduct the sensing interviews in phase IV, I suggest you share the three lowest (best) scores and review a few questionnaire items from those categories. The following discussion is representative of how this may be handled.

"Your team's average score in category II, Unqualified Leadership, was .02. Such a low score indicates that almost everyone on your team felt that items 2, 14, 26, 30, etc., did *not* accurately describe your team.

In other words, there is a high level of mutual respect between and among your teammates for the skills and qualifications; this is clearly a strength of your team. As we conduct the team building workshop, we will build on the strengths while addressing the areas of concern.

However, your team's average score on categories IX, Soft Critiquing, was 7.6, which indicates many respondents felt items 9, 21, 33, 44, etc., *do* accurately describe your teams. Do you feel this assessment is valid, and if so, how do you suggest we deal with this area of concern?"

The process of sharing the strengths and the opportunities for growth during these interviews is very helpful in preparing the group for the team-building workshop in phase VII.

TEAM-REVIEW QUESTIONNAIRE ANSWER SHEET

- Follow the instructions at the beginning of the questionnaire.

- In the grid shown here there are 108 squares, each one numbered to correspond to the statements on the questionnaire.

- If you think a statement is broadly true about your team, mark an X through the square. If you feel a statement is not broadly true, then leave the square blank.

- Fill in the top line first, working from left to right; then fill in the second line, etc.

- Be careful to respond to each statement, but mark an asterisk next to the numbers of statements that you find especially significant or difficult to answer. These can be explored later.

Answer Grid

1	2	3	4	5	6	7	8	9	10	11	12
13	14	15	16	17	18	19	20	21	22	23	24
25	26	27	28	29	30	31	32	33	34	35	36
37	38	39	40	41	42	43	44	45	46	47	48
49	50	51	52	53	54	55	56	57	58	59	60
61	62	63	64	65	66	67	68	69	70	71	72
73	74	75	76	77	78	79	80	81	82	83	84
85	86	87	88	89	90	91	92	93	94	95	96
97	98	99	100	101	102	103	104	105	106	107	108

Totals

I	II	III	IV	V	VI	VII	VIII	IX	X	XI	XII

TEAM REVIEW QUESTIONNAIRE
INTERPRETATION SHEET

	Your Team	Your Ranking	Team Average	Team Ranking	
I					Inappropriate Leadership
II					Unqualified Membership
III					Insufficient Group Commitment
IV					Unconstructive Climate
V					Low Achievement Orientation
VI					Undeveloped Corporate Role
VII					Ineffective Work Methods
VIII					Inadequate Team Organization
IX					Soft Critiquing
X					Stunted Individual Development
XI					Lack of Creative Capacity
XII					Negative Intergroup Relations

Appendix D

Departmental Conflict Resolution

(see Chapter 3 and 6)

On occasion you will find destructive conflict between two or more departments and/or the department heads. The following process is somewhat time consuming but has been extremely effective in breaking down communication barriers which impair effective teamwork.

1. Assemble the entire management team with 2 or 3 people from each department. In most organizations the total group should average 20-30 in size.

2. Distribute worksheets to each department head, one for each department except the person's own (see attached).

3. Ask the representatives from each department to go to a separate room and complete the attached Department/Team Feedback forms.

Department/Team

Feedback

Date_____

From: _____Department

To: _____Department

I. We value and appreciate the following: (be specific, not general)

   a. Continue...

   b. We would like to see more ...

   c. Please start doing ...

II. We do not value or appreciate the following (be specific, not general)

   a. Please stop...

   b. We would like to see less ...

   c. What we need from you to be successful is...

Appendix E

"Knowledge for Teams"
An Assessment Tool

===========

In our discussion of the solution for the performance problem " lack of skill or knowledge," we stressed to train against the deficit. In other words, don't waste time and money teaching what the team already knows or does not need. Teach what they need and do not know.

In my years of management consulting, I have come in contact with scores of companies and consultants offering a plethora of assessment instruments and training materials.

Edge Training Systems, led by Paul O'Keefe in Richmond, VA, has developed the best and most cost-effective team assessment tool I have seen to date.

With only eighty-nine multiple-choice questions, their "Knowledge for Teams" instrument measures each team member's as well as the entire team's collective knowledge in six key areas:

COMMUNICATION   Effective oral communication among team members

COORDINATION   Preparing and planning for success in achieving team goals and objectives

COLLABORATION   Skills for holding effective team meetings, training team members, making decisions together, and solving problems

COOPERATION   Negotiating differences and managing conflict within the team

CHANGE   Managing and adapting to organizational change

COACHING   Team leadership and coaching skills

The feedback reports are concise and user friendly. The Cumulative Group Report provides percentage of questions correct, the group's range and average score, the percentile rank compared to every respondent who has ever completed the assessment plus the "strengths and needs" in each of the six areas.

This excellent tool is a state-of-the-art team assessment instrument I highly recommend. A call to Edge Training Systems, Inc. at 1-800-476-1405 will serve you well.

ENDNOTES

Chapter 1
Katzenbach, Jon R. and Douglas K, Smith. *The Wisdom of Teams.* (New York: Harper Collins, 1994) 45.

Chapter 2
Jackson, Phil and Delehanty Hugh. *Sacred Hoops.* (New York: Hyperior, 1995) 21.

Chapter 4
"Nothin' But A Winner" Video featuring Coach Paul "Bear" Bryant. (Niles, IL: United Training Media).

Leatherman, Dr. Dick. "Motivating Employees Module." (Richmond: International Training Consultants, Inc. , 1996).

Chapter 5
Thomas, K. V. *Conflict and Conflict Management* Working Paper #74-3.
Leatherman, Dr. Dick. "Taking Disciplinary Action Module." (Richmond: International Training Consultants, Inc. , 1996).

Chapter 6

O'Keefe, Paul. "Knowledge For Teams" Assessment Tool. (Richmond: Edge Training Systems, Inc. 1998).

Francis, Dave and Young, Don. *Improving Work Groups.* (San Diego: University Associates, Inc. 1992) 42-52.